Revolutions In Reverse

DAVID GRAEBER

Revolutions in Reverse: Essays on Politics, Violence, Art, and Imagination
David Graeber

ISBN 978-1-57027-243-1

Cover design by Haduhi Szukis
Interior layout by Margaret Killjoy

Released by Minor Compositions, London / New York / Port Watson
Minor Compositions is a series of interventions & provocations
drawing from autonomous politics, avant-garde aesthetics, and the
revolutions of everyday life.

Minor Compositions is an imprint of Autonomedia
www.minorcompositions.info | info@minorcompositions.info

Distributed by Autonomedia
PO Box 568 Williamsburgh Station
Brooklyn, NY 11211

Phone/fax: 718-963-0568
www.autonomedia.org info@autonomedia.org

Contents

Introduction

THE EDITORS HAVE ASKED ME, NOT UNREASONABLY, TO PRO-
vide a brief introduction explaining how all these essays hang together. It's an interesting question because it wasn't my idea to
combine them all in the same volume to begin with. Actually,
the collection first came out in Greek, with the title *Κίνημα, βία,
τέχνη και επανάσταση* (*Movement, Violence, Art and Revolution*.
Athens: Black Pepper Press, 2009), and they were assembled by
their editor, and translator, Spyros Koyroyklis. When I first saw
the volume on a visit to Greece in May of 2010 I thought the idea
for the collection was inspired; it made a sort of intuitive sense
to me; as did it, I was soon given to understand, to many in the
movement in Greece itself, where many of the arguments found
within were taken up by various anarchists, anti-authoritarians,
and activists in the wake of the economic crisis and confusion that
followed the heady days of December 2009.

So what is the unifying theme?

It's helpful, perhaps, to consider the context in which these essays were originally written. All of these essays were composed
between 2004 and 2010. This was not an easy time for someone, like myself, actively engaged in social movements. Between
roughly 1998 and 2002, the advent of the global justice movement
had given all of us a sudden sense of almost endless possibility.

The wake of 9/11 threw everything into disarray. For many it was impossible to maintain the sense of enthusiasm that had kept us so alive in the years before; many burned out, gave up, emigrated, bickered, killed themselves, applied to graduate school, or withdrew into various other sorts of morbid desperation. For me, the point where I came closest to despair was in the immediate wake of the 2004 US elections, when the originally stolen presidency of George W. Bush was actually given what seemed like a genuine popular mandate. At first, in the immediate aftermath of 9/11, it seemed that we were looking at a repeat of something rather like World War I: the period from roughly 1880 to 1914 was after all quite similar to the decade and a piece that followed the fall of the Berlin Wall: a time where wars between major powers seemed to be a thing of the past, where the dominant powers embraced an ethos of free trade and free markets, of frenetic capital accumulation, but at the same time, an age of the rapid rise of global anticapitalist movements, accompanied by an ethos of revolutionary internationalism in which the anarchist movement seemed to define the vital center of the radical left. The rulers of the world ultimately panicked, and reacted by initiating a near-century of world war, allowing appeals to nationalism, state security, racism and jingoism of every kind of tear those (to it) terrifying alliances apart. It struck me, after 9/11, that they were trying the same trick again; it was as if, faced with even the prospect of an effective anticapitalist movement emerging globally, they immediately pulled out the biggest gun they had – a declaration of permanent global war mobilization – despite the fact that the enemy they had chosen, rag-tag band of Islamists who had, effectively, got extraordinarily lucky, pulling off one of the first mad terrorist schemes in history that had actually worked, and were clearly never going to repeat the performance – could not possibly provide an adequate long-term excuse. It was never going to work. Yet somehow, the American public had passed a referendum on the project. What's more, I watched in dismay how every attempt to revive an international spirit resistance – around the G8, then G20, the Climate Conferences – seemed to founder, or at least, reach a series of limited tactic victories that always seemed to hold out the promise of translating into a new burst of energy and of longer-term movement building ("finally," we kept telling each other, "we're over the hump!"), but which, in reality, never really did. In part, yes, it was because the level of repression – or more precisely, what the police and other security forces felt they could get away with in dealing with us – had dramatically increased. But that was by no means all of it. To the contrary, it was the enemy's very disorganization that was our worst foil.

I especially remember when, in 2007, before the G-8 meetings in Japan, some Japanese friends asked me to put together a strategic analysis of the global situation from the perspective of capital, and the movements against it. I ended up working with a brilliant team, mainly drawn from people active in the Midnight Notes collective – and we developed what I still consider a compelling analysis of the economic impasse faced by capital at that moment and the most plausible strategy to overcome it. (Essentially, we expected them to a declare of global ecological crisis, followed by a green capitalist strategy designed to divert resources like sovereign wealth funds beginning to slip away from the control of financial elites back under their control.) I still hold it was the best strategy they could have adopted from the perspective of the long-term viability of the capitalist order. Problem was: that clearly wasn't their priority. At the summits, all they did was bicker with one another. What's the radical response to confusion? How on earth were we able to come up with a response to their evil plans if they couldn't even figure out what those were?

Of course in retrospect, it's easier to see what was happening. Those bigwigs assembling at their various summits were probably more aware than we were that the entire system – based on a very old-fashioned alliance of military and financial power typical of the latter days of capitalist empires – was being held together with tape and string. They were less concerned to save the system, than to ensure that there remained no plausible alternative in anyone's mind so that, when the moment of collapse did come, they would be the only one's offering solutions. Not that since the great financial collapse of 2008, solutions have been particularly forthcoming. But at least there is no way to deny now that a fundamental problem does exist. The order that existed between 2004 and 2008 – even if it has managed to achieve a kind of grudging acquiescence in critical quarters of the world – is never coming back. It simply wasn't viable.

These essays then are the product of a confused interregnum. It was a time when it was very difficult to find signs of hope. If there is a single theme in this collection of essays, then, it is that they all start out from some aspect of the period that seems particularly bleak, depressing, what appeared to be some failure, stumbling block, countervailing force, foolishness of the global anticapitalist movement, and to try to recuperate something, some hidden aspect we usually don't notice, some angle from which the same apparently desolate landscape might look entirely different.

This is most obvious perhaps in the first three essays, all of which concern the lessons to be learned from the global justice movement; but it's true, in one way or another, of all of them.

It's appropriate, then, that the collection begins with *The Shock of Victory*, which is perhaps the most explicit in this regard. Most of us who had been involved in the global justice movement did not, as I remarked, come out of it feeling we had made much of dent in the world. We all experienced the infighting and frazzled confusion that followed the first heady years, the crumbling alliances and seemingly endless bitter arguments over racism, sexism, privilege, lifestyle, "summit-hopping," process, the lack of ties to genuine communities in resistance... And we saw it as the proof of our ultimate fecklessness as a movement, our failure to achieve any of our major goals. The irony is that, really, all these things were a direct result of our success. Most of the squabbling was really slightly an indirect way of conducting strategic debates about what to do now that we had achieved so many of our immediate goals – to end structural adjustment policies and block new global trade agreements, halt the growth and blunt the power of institutions of neoliberal governance like the IMF and WTO – had been achieved so quickly. The problem was that almost no one actually recognized them as such, which made it almost impossible to conduct a full and honest debate, and the intensity of the arguments and resulting frustration became so overwhelming that almost no one seemed to notice we'd achieved our goals in the first place! True, the essay ends by posing a much a larger question, as *Turbulence* magazine was to phrase it in a special issue a year or two later, "What would it mean to win?" But largely it is a comment on the extraordinary historical effectiveness of movements based on direct action and direct democracy, and the curious fact that our enemies (as their panic reactions seem to indicate) seem recognize the potential effectiveness of such movements, the threat they pose to global power relations, much more than those active in the movements themselves do.

Hope in Common takes up the same theme and pushes it even further. What if the reason why those who would like to see a world organized by some principle other than capitalism feel so depressed most of the time is because capitalists, and politicians, have become veritably obsessed with making us feel that way? Perhaps the real meaning of neoliberalism is precisely that. Neoliberal capitalism is that form that is utterly obsessed with ensuring that it seems that, as Margaret Thatcher so famously declared in the 1980s, "there is no alternative." In other words, it has largely given up on any serious effort to argue that the current economic order is actually a good order, just, reasonable, that it will ever prove capable of creating a world in which most human beings feel prosperous, safe, and free to spend any significant portion of their life pursuing those things they consider genuinely important. Rather, it is a terrible system, in which even the very richest countries cannot guarantee access to such basic needs as health and education to the majority of their citizens, it works badly, but no other system could possibly work at all. (It's actually quite fascinating how quickly, at the end of the Cold War, the language used to describe the Soviet Union shifted. Obviously, no sane person could wish for a restoration of such a system, and we are very unlikely to ever see one. All this is good. But at the same time, rhetoric shifted almost overnight from declaring that a top down command economy with no market forces could not compete effectively with the most advanced capitalist powers, either militarily or economically, to the absolute, dismissive assurance that communism "just doesn't work" – effectively, that no such system could ever have existed at all. It seems a remarkable conclusion, considering that the Soviet Union did in fact exist, for over 70 years, and took Russia within decades from a laughable backwater to a major technological and military power.)

All this remained a bit obscure in the years surrounding the end of the Cold War, when overenthusiastic neoliberal "reformers" were fancying themselves revolutionaries, and everyone felt that microcredit was about to turn the world's poor into prosperous entrepreneurs. But in the years since the neoliberal project really has been stripped down to what was always its essence: not an economic project at all, but a political project, designed to devastate the imagination, and willing – with it's cumbersome securitization and insane military projects – to destroy the capitalist order itself if that's what it took to make it seem inevitable. Behind our feeling of helplessness, then, there is a gargantuan, and extraordinarily expensive engine that is ultimately likely to crush the current system under its own dead weight.

The final essay of the set, *Revolution in Reverse*, considers the stakes of this war on the imagination on a deeper level. It has a curious history. The piece was originally commissioned for a special issue of *New Left Review*, the editor playing a hands-on role in shaping its overall structure; then, a year later, rejected out of hand without even allowing me a chance to respond to criticism (the editors of *New Left Review*, being essentially aristocrats, are notorious for this sort of high-handed behavior.) The only comments I did get were – well, they didn't quite put it this way, but very nearly – that English-speaking authors have no business trying to come up with original theoretical formulations; such things are properly left to speakers of German, Italian, or French. (Our role, apparently, is simply to provide appropriate commentary.)

Well, whether or not it is my place to engage in theoretical reflection, this is what I did here. These are reflections born of years of work with the Direct Action Network and other anarchist-inspired groups, which confronts another point of apparent despair for contemporary radicals: Whatever happened to The Revolution? For much of the 19th and early 20th centuries, even most capitalists in countries like the US or Germany seemed to harbor the strong suspicion that, any day now, they might all end up hanging from trees; nowadays, few revolutionaries seem to be able to imagine it. What, then, does being a revolutionary actually mean? A great deal, is the answer, since the old apocalyptic version of revolution – the victorious battles in the streets, the spontaneous outpouring of popular festivity, the creation of new democratic institutions, the ultimate reinvention of life itself – never quite seemed to work itself out, and there is no particular reason to imagine it ever could have. It's not that any of these dreams have ever gone away, or reason to believe they ever could either. It's that, between the anarchist insistence that we can no longer imagine revolution solely within the framework of the nation-state, and even more, the feminist insistence that how we treat each other in working to make the revolution, particularly in its most apparently humdrum and unromantic moments, is what will ultimately determine whether we have any chance of creating a world worth living in, whatever the final, tactical victory might look like, we have begun to rearrange the pieces. The great mobilizations of Seattle, Prague, Genoa, or the constant direct actions in places like Greece, Chiapas or South Korea, have effectively operated by taking all the familiar stages of revolution and simply turning the traditional order on its head. Understand the full implications of this shift, in turn, demands some major work in re-imagination what terms like violence, alienation, "realism" itself actually mean.

The next two essays might seem different in nature, but really they are doing much the same work. Each searches for redemption in what might otherwise seem like an abyss. It's more obvious perhaps in the case of the first, *Army of Altruists*. This essay grew directly out of a feeling of hopeless intellectual frustration. I had woken up on Wednesday, November 4th, 2004 to learn that George W. Bush had been reelected President of the USA, in an election that, apparently, wasn't even stolen. At the time I was due to teach a graduate seminar in a course called "Anthropology and Classical Social Theory" at Yale – the topic that morning was supposed to be on Max Weber's theories of religion. None of us really felt up to it. Instead, the class turned into a prolonged and sometimes agonized discussion of the relevance of social theory itself: was there really a point, then, to what we did, or were being trained to do? Does Theory – the sort that begins with a capital "T" – really afford us a better vantage from which to understand what had just happened, particularly, why so many working class people had voted in a manner that seemed diametrically opposed to their own class interests, than ordinary common sense might afford? And if not, what were we really doing by pursuing careers in the academy? We didn't come up with any strong conclusions (though we did end up having an interesting discussion of the possibility of breaking the US landmass up into separate territories, merging some with Canada and others with Mexico, and even produced some stickers that said 'No Longer Under US Jurisdiction'). But the question didn't go away; it continued to trouble me. It was all the more so because there was no consensus, at the time, that theory was all that important. I had spent a number of perfectly good years of my life, for instance, working frenetically researching and typing away at a book about anthropological value theory – being convinced, at the time, that doing so was almost a kind of intellectual duty, unleashing on the world powerful theoretical developments that had been crafted in University of Chicago at the time I was there, and whose authors, I had always felt rather irresponsibly, had never published in any sort of broadly accessible form. The result was, I felt, a major contribution to the discipline. When I did publish it, in 2001, I found the discipline did not agree. No one paid much attention to it, and I was greeted with the distinct feeling that University-of-Chicago-style grand theorizing of this sort was itself considered irrelevant and passé. Could it be anthropologists were right to move on?

Well, I managed to answer the question to my own satisfaction anyway. The application of theory was indeed able to reveal things that would not otherwise have been obvious. What it mainly revealed was that one of the most insidious of the "hidden injuries of class" in North American society was the denial of the right to do good, to be noble, to pursue any form of value other than money – or, at least, to do it and to gain any financial security or rewards for having done. The passionate hatred of the "liberal elite" among right-wing populists came down, in practice, to the utterly justified resentment towards a class that had sequestered, for its own children, every opportunity to pursue love, truth, beauty, honor, decency, and to be afforded the means to exist while doing so. The endless identification with soldiers ("support our troops!) – that is, with individuals who have, over the years, been reduced to little more than high tech mercenaries enforcing of a global regime of financial capital – lay in the fact that these are almost the only individuals of working class origin in the US who have figured out a way to get paid for pursuing some kind of higher ideal, or at least being able to imagine that's what they're doing. Obviously most would prefer to pursue higher ideals in way that did not involve the risk of having their legs blown off. The sense of rage, in fact, stems above all from the knowledge that all such jobs are taken by children of the rich. It's a strangely ambivalent picture, and one that, at this moment of revival of right-wing populism, we might do well to consider once again.

The *Sadness of Postworkerism* begins with a group of people who might seem the epitome of everything a right-wing populist detests: a group of former '60s revolutionaries, now being paid to lecture on art history to an audience of gallery owners and grad students at London's Tate Museum in fall 2006. The element redemption here is partly that when you actually meet such people, they are hardly the egotistical prima donnas one imagines. Actually, they appeared to be sincere, decent sorts of people, who would really much rather have been standing arm to arm with proletarian rebels at the barricades, and as confused as anyone how they had ended up explaining art trends to dilettantes. Much of essay is, again, a theoretical reflection – not so much of my own theories as those elements of '70s Italian revolutionary theory that have made their way into the English-speaking academy and art world in recent years, and the assessment is pretty unsparing. Still the main critique is not so much that this particular strain of post-Workerist thought is wrong so much as that it's misplaced, we are not dealing with theory at all here, but prophecy, and the attempt to unravel what's really happening here – both on the level of ideas, of what happens to intellectual traditions when they would seem to have thoroughly exhausted their radical possibilities, and in the art world itself, even within those peculiar domains where art blends into fashion, and both most are firmly wedded to financial abstraction, there are peculiar domains of freedom that transcend the dead hand of capital. Ultimately, "the revolution," however conceived, can never really go away, because the notion of a redemptive future remains the only way we can possibly make sense of the present; we can only understand the value of what surrounds us from the perspective of an imaginary country whose own contours we can never understand, even when we are standing in it.

The last essay, *Against Kamakaze Capitalism*, was not part of the Greek collection; it was written afterwards; quite recently, in fact, in the fall of 2010. But I think it belongs here. More directly concerned with questions of revolutionary strategy than most, it also considers such questions in the light of that very situation of impasse – and of the murder of dreams – that has haunted so much of this collection. Here, too, the argument sets off with hope from an unexpected quarter: a surprising convergence, and recognition of a common cause, between climate protestors and petroleum workers during the French strike wave of October 2010. Many of the greatest cleavages we imagine to exist within the movements ranged against capitalism at the moment – the one between the ecological, direct action movement, and trade unionists, "hippies and hardhats" as they called them in the '60s, or "Teamsters and Turtles" as they called them during one previous instance of apparently serendipitous alliance in Seattle in 1999 – might not be nearly such a cleavage as we imagine. The working class has always been torn between what's basically a petty bourgeois productivist ideology (or if you prefer, productivist/consumerist ideology, since it's obvious two sides of the same coin), and a much more fundamental rejection of the very principle of work as it exists in our society – an urge which its "respectable" leaders have spent most of the last century trying to stifle, denounce, or pretend not to exist. At a moment when the capitalists' collective refusal to even consider rethinking any of their basic assumptions about the world might well mean not just the death of capitalism, but of almost everything else, our only real choice is do it ourselves – to begin to create a new language, a new common sense, about what people basically are and what it is reasonable for them to expect from the world, and from each other. A case could well be made that the fate of the world depends on it.

That's what this volume really is. It's my own attempt – however modest, however hesitant – to start such a conversation, and most of all, to suggest that the task might not be nearly so daunting as we'd be given to imagine.

The Shock of Victory

THE BIGGEST PROBLEM FACING DIRECT ACTION MOVEMENTS IS that we don't know how to handle victory.

This might seem an odd thing to say because of a lot of us haven't been feeling particularly victorious of late. Most anarchists today feel the global justice movement was kind of a blip: inspiring, certainly, while it lasted, but not a movement that succeeded either in putting down lasting organizational roots or transforming the contours of power in the world. The anti-war movement after September 11, 2001 was even more frustrating, since anarchists, and anarchist tactics, were largely marginalized. The war will end, of course, but that's just because wars always do. No one is feeling they contributed much to it.

I want to suggest an alternative interpretation. Let me lay out three initial propositions here:

1) Odd though it may seem, the ruling classes live in fear of us. They appear to still be haunted by the possibility that, if average Americans really get wind of what they're up to, they might all end up hanging from trees. It know it seems implausible but it's hard to come up with any other explanation for the way they go into panic mode the moment there is any sign of mass mobilization, and especially mass

direct action, and usually try to distract attention by starting some kind of war.

2) In a way this panic is justified. Mass direct action – especially when it is organized on directly democratic lines – is incredibly effective. Over the last thirty years in America, there have been only two instances of mass action of this sort: the anti-nuclear movement in the late '70s, and the so called "anti-globalization" movement from roughly 1999-2001.[1] In each case, the movement's main political goals were reached far more quickly than almost anyone involved imagined possible.

3) The real problem such movements face is that they always get taken by surprise by the speed of their initial success. We are never prepared for victory. It throws us into confusion. We start fighting each other. The government invariably responds by some sort of military adventurism overseas. The ratcheting of repression and appeals to nationalism that inevitably accompanies a new round of war mobilization then plays into the hands of authoritarians on every side of the political spectrum. As a result, by the time the full impact of our initial victory becomes clear, we're usually too busy feeling like failures to even notice it.

Let me take these two most prominent examples case by case:

I: The Anti-Nuclear Movement

THE ANTI-NUCLEAR MOVEMENT of the late '70s marked the first appearance in North America of what we now consider standard anarchist tactics and forms of organization: mass actions, affinity groups, spokescouncils, consensus process, jail solidarity, the very principle of decentralized direct democracy. It was all somewhat

---

1   If one were to extend the temporal range to the last 50 years, we could also include the Civil Rights movement, where the SNCC (Student Non-Violent Coordinating Committee) branch of the movement was also consensus-based and anti-authoritarian. It followed the same broad pattern, except, of course, that its victories were much harder to deny.

primitive, compared to now, and there were significant differences – notably a much stricter, Gandhian-style conceptions of non-violence – but all the elements were there and it was the first time they had come together as a package. For two years, the movement grew with amazing speed and showed every sign of becoming a nation-wide phenomenon. Then almost as quickly, it distintegrated.

It all began when, in 1974, some veteran peaceniks turned organic farmers in New England successfully blocked construction of a proposed nuclear power plant in Montague, Massachusetts. In 1976, they joined with other New England activists, inspired by the success of a year-long plant occupation in Germany, to create the Clamshell Alliance. Clamshell's immediate goal was to stop construction of a proposed nuclear power plant in Seabrook, New Hampshire. While the alliance never ended up managing an occupation so much as a series of dramatic mass-arrests, combined with jail solidarity, their actions – involving, at peak, tens of thousands of people organized on directly democratic lines – succeeded in throwing the very idea of nuclear power into question in a way it had never been before. Similar coalitions began springing up across the country: the Palmetto alliance in South Carolina, Oystershell in Maryland, Sunflower in Kansas, and most famous of all, the Abalone Alliance in California, reacting originally to an insane plan to build a nuclear power plant at Diablo Canyon, almost directly on top of a major geographic fault line.

Clamshell first three mass actions, in 1976 and 1977, were wildly successful. But it soon fell into crisis over questions of democratic process. In May 1978, a newly created Coordinating Committee violated process to accept a last-minute government offer for a three-day legal rally at Seabrook instead of a planned fourth occupation (the excuse was reluctance to alienate the surrounding community). Acrimonious debates began about consensus and community relations, which then expanded to the role of non-violence (even cutting through fences, or defensive measures like gas masks, had originally been forbidden), gender bias, race and class privilege, and so on. By 1979 the alliance had split into two contending, and increasingly ineffective, factions, and after many delays, the Seabrook plant (or half of it anyway) did go into operation. The Abalone Alliance lasted longer, until 1985, in part because its strong core of anarcha-feminists, but in the end, Diablo Canyon too won its license and came online in December 1988.

Tell the story this way, it doesn't seem particularly inspiring. But there is another way to tell it. We could ask: what was the movement really trying to achieve?

It might helpful here to map out its full range of goals:

1) **Short-Term Goals**: to block construction of the particular nuclear plant in question (Seabrook, Diablo Canyon...)

2) **Medium-Term Goals**: to block construction of all new nuclear plants, delegitimize the very idea of nuclear power and begin moving towards conservation and green power, and legitimate new forms of non-violent resistance and feminist-inspired direct democracy

3) **Long-Term Goals**: (at least for the more radical elements) smash the state and destroy capitalism

If so the results are clear. Short-term goals were almost never reached. Despite numerous tactical victories (delays, utility company bankruptcies, legal injunctions) the plants that became the focus of mass action all ultimately went on line. Governments simply cannot allow themselves to be seen to lose in such a battle. Long-term goals were also obviously not obtained. But one reason they weren't is that the medium-term goals were all reached almost immediately. The actions did delegitimize the very idea of nuclear power – raising public awareness to the point that when Three Mile Island melted down in 1979, it doomed the industry forever. While plans for Seabrook and Diablo Canyon might not have been cancelled, just about every other then-pending plan to build a nuclear reactor was, and no new ones have been proposed for a quarter century. There was indeed a more towards conservation, green power, and a legitimizing of new democratic organizing techniques. All this happened much more quickly than anyone had really anticipated.

In retrospect, it's easy to see most of the subsequent problems emerged directly from the very speed of the movement's success. Radicals had hoped to make links between the nuclear industry and the very nature of the capitalist system that created it. As it turns out, the capitalist system proved more than willing to jettison the nuclear industry the moment it became a liability. Once giant utility companies began claiming they too wanted to promote green energy, effectively inviting what we'd now call the NGO types to a space at the table, there was an enormous temptation to jump ship. Especially because many of them had only allied with more radical groups so as to win themselves a place at the table to begin with.

The inevitable result was a series of heated strategic debates. It's impossible to understand this, though, without first understanding that strategic debates, within directly democratic movements, are rarely conducted *as* strategic debates. They almost always pretend to be arguments about something else. Take for instance the question of capitalism. Anticapitalists are usually more than happy to discuss their position on the subject. Liberals on the other hand really don't like being forced to say "actually, I am in favor of maintaining capitalism in some form or another'" – so whenever possible, they try to change the subject. Consequently, debates that are actually about whether to directly challenge capitalism usually end up getting argued out as if they were short-term debates about tactics and non-violence. Authoritarian socialists or others who are suspicious of democracy are rarely keen on having to make that an issue either, and prefer to discuss the need to create the broadest possible coalitions. Those who do support the principle of direct democracy but feel a group is taking the wrong strategic direction often find it much more effective to challenge its decision-making process than to challenge its actual decisions.

There is another factor here that is even less remarked, but I think equally important. Everyone knows that faced with a broad and potentially revolutionary coalition, any governments' first move will be to try to split it. Making concessions to placate the moderates while selectively criminalizing the radicals – this is Art of Governance 101. The US government, though has an additional weapon most governments do not. It is in possession of a global empire, permanently mobilized for war. Those running it can, pretty much any time they like, decide to ratchet up the level of violence overseas. This has proved a remarkably effective way to defuse social movements founded around domestic concerns. It seems no coincidence that the civil rights movement was followed by major political concessions *and* a rapid escalation of the

war in Vietnam; that the anti-nuclear movement was followed by
the abandonment of nuclear power *and* a ramping up of the Cold
War, with Star Wars programs and proxy wars in Afghanistan and
Central America; that the global justice movement was followed
by the collapse of the Washington consensus *and* the Global War
on Terror. As a result SDS had to put aside its early emphasis on
participatory democracy to become an organizer of anti-war protests; the anti-nuclear movement was obliged to morph into a
nuclear freeze movement; the horizontal structures of DAN and
PGA gave way to top-down mass organizations like ANSWER and
UFPJ. Granted, from the government's point of view the military
solution does have its risks. The whole thing can blow up in one's
face, as it did in Vietnam (hence the obsession, at least since the
first Gulf War to design a war that was effectively protest-proof.)
There is also always a small risk some miscalculation will acciden-
tally trigger a nuclear Armageddon and destroy the planet. But
these are risks politicians faced with civil unrest appear to have
normally been more than willing to take – if only because directly democratic movements genuinely scare them, while anti-war
movements are their preferred adversary. States are, after all, ultimately forms of violence. For them, changing the argument to one
about violence is taking things back to their home turf, the kind
of things they really prefer to talk about. Organizations designed
either to wage, or to oppose, wars will always tend to be more hi-
erarchically organized than those designed with almost anything
else in mind. This is certainly what happened in the case of the
anti-nuclear movement. While the anti-war mobilizations of the
'80s turned out far larger numbers than Clamshell or Abalone
ever had, they also marked a return to the days of marching along
with signs, permitted rallies, and abandoning experiments with
new tactics and new forms of direct democracy.

II: The Global justice movement

I'LL ASSUME OUR gentle reader is broadly familiar with the actions at Seattle, IMF-World Bank blockades six months later in
Washington at A16, and so on.

In the US, the movement flared up so quickly and dramatically
even the media could not completely dismiss it. It also quickly began to eat itself. Direct Action Networks were founded in almost

every major city in America. While some of these (notably Seattle and Los Angeles DAN) were reformist, "anti-corporate," and fans of non-violence codes of non-violence, most (like New York and Chicago DAN) were overwhelmingly anarchist and anticapitalist, and dedicated to the principle of "diversity of tactics." Other cities (Montreal, Washington D.C.) created even more explicitly anarchist Anticapitalist Convergences. These groups had different fates. The anti-corporate DANs dissolved almost immediately, the anticapitalist ones endured longer, but even among those, very few were still around even four years later. They were all wracked almost from the beginning with bitter debates: about non-violence, about summit-hopping, about racism and privilege issues,[2] about the viability of the network model. Then there was 9/11, followed by a huge increase up of the level of repression and resultant paranoia, and the panicked flight of almost all our former allies among unions and NGOs. At this point the debates became downright paralyzing. By Miami, in 2003, it seemed like we'd been put to rout, and despite periodic surges of enthusiasm (Gleneagles, Minneapolis, Heilengendam) the movement never really recovered.

Again, the story seems uninspiring. And here's there's the added factor of 9/11. September 11th, after all, was such a weird event, such a catastrophe, but also such an historical fluke, that it almost blinds us to everything that was going on around it. In the immediate aftermath of the attacks, almost all of the structures created during the globalization movement collapsed. But one reason it was so easy for them to collapse was – not just that war and anti-war mobilizations seemed such an immediately more pressing concern – but that once again, in most of our immediate objectives, we'd already, unexpectedly, won.

Myself, I joined NYC DAN right around the time of A16. At that time, DAN as a whole saw itself as a group with two major

---

2   Incidentally, this is not to say that issues of racism and privilege are unimportant. I feel a little silly even having to say this, but it would seem that, within the movement, anything one writes that might be taken to imply one does not take such issues seriously will be interpreted that way. What I would argue is that the *way* that racial and class have been debated in the movement appear to have been startling ineffective in overcoming racial divisions in the movement, and I suspect this is at least partially because these debates are, in fact, veiled ways of arguing about something else.

objectives. One was to help coordinate the North American wing of a vast global movement against neoliberalism, and what was then called the Washington Consensus, to destroy the hegemony of neoliberal ideas, stop all the new big trade agreements (WTO, FTAA), and to discredit and eventually destroy organizations like the IMF. The other was to disseminate a (very much anarchist-inspired) model of direct democracy: decentralized, affinity-group structures, consensus process, to replace old-fashioned activist organizing styles with their steering committees and ideological squabbles. At the time we sometimes called it "contamination-ism," the idea that all people really needed was to be exposed to the experience of direct action and direct democracy, and they would want to start imitating it all by themselves. There was a general feeling that we weren't trying to build a permanent structure; DAN was just a means to this end. When it had served its purpose, several founding members explained to me, there would be no further need for it. On the other hand these were pretty ambitious goals, so we also assumed even if we did attain them, it would probably take at least a decade.

As it turned out, it took about a year and a half.

Obviously, we failed to spark a social revolution. But one reason we never got to the point of inspiring hundreds of thousands of people across the world to rise up was, again, that we had achieved so many of our other goals so quickly. Take the question of organization. While the anti-war coalitions still operate, as anti-war coalitions always do, as top-down popular front groups, almost every small-scale radical group that isn't dominated by Marxist sectarians of some sort or another – and this includes anything from organizations of Syrian immigrants in Montreal or community gardens in Detroit – now operate on largely anarchist principles. They might not know it. But contaminationism worked. Alternately, take the domain of ideas. The Washington consensus lies in ruins. So much so, it's hard now to remember what public discourse in this country before Seattle was even like. Myself, I remember quite well. Consider the issue of "free trade," the ostensible focus of the protests. ("Free trade" is obviously a propaganda term, but it was significant in itself that in America, this was the only term available to refer to neoliberal globalization.) I don't believe there was ever a time when both the mainstream media and the political classes had been ever so completely unanimous about anything. That "free trade," "free markets," and no-holds-barred supercharged capitalism were the only possible direction for human history, the only possible solution for any problem was so completely taken for granted that anyone who cast doubt on the proposition was treated as literally insane. Global justice activists, when they first forced themselves into the attention of CNN or Newsweek, were immediately written off as reactionary "flat-earthers," whose opposition to free trade could only be explained by childish ignorance of the most elementary principles of economics. A year later, CNN and Newsweek were saying, effectively, "all right, well maybe the kids have won the argument."

Usually when I make this point in front of anarchist crowds someone immediately objects: "well, sure, the rhetoric has changed, but the policies remain the same."

I suppose this is true in a manner of speaking. And certainly it's true that we didn't destroy capitalism. But we (taking the "we" here as the horizontalist, direct-action oriented wing of the planetary movement against neoliberalism) did arguably deal it a bigger blow in just two years than anyone since, say, the Russian Revolution.

Let me take this point by point

- **FREE TRADE AGREEMENTS**. All the ambitious free trade treaties planned since 1998 have failed, the MAI was routed; the FTAA, focus of the actions in Quebec City and Miami, stopped dead in its tracks. Most of us remember the 2003 FTAA summit mainly for introducing the "Miami model" of extreme police repression even against obviously non-violent civil resistance. It was that. But we forget this was more than anything the enraged flailings of a pack of extremely sore losers – Miami was the meeting where the FTAA was definitively killed. Now no one is even talking about broad, ambitious treaties on that scale. The US is reduced to pushing for minor country-to-country trade pacts with traditional allies like South Korea and Peru, or at best deals like CAFTA, uniting its remaining client states in Central America, and it's not even clear it will manage to pull off that.

- **THE WORLD TRADE ORGANIZATION.** After the catastrophe (for them) in Seattle, organizers moved the next meeting to the Persian Gulf island of Doha, apparently deciding they would rather run the risk of being blown up by Osama bin Laden than having to face another DAN blockade. For six years they hammered away at the "Doha round." The problem was that, emboldened by the protest movement, Southern governments began insisting they would no longer agree open their borders to agricultural imports from rich countries unless those rich countries at least stopped pouring billions of dollars of subsidies at their own farmers, thus ensuring Southern farmers couldn't possibly compete. Since the US in particular had no intention of itself making any of the sort of sacrifices it demanded of others, all deals were off. In July 2006, Pierre Lamy, head of the WTO, declared the Doha round dead and at this point no one is even talking about another WTO negotiation for at least two years – some speculated that ultimately, the organization itself might cease to exist.

- **THE INTERNATIONAL MONETARY FUND AND WORLD BANK.** This is the most amazing story of all. By 2008, the IMF was rapidly approaching bankruptcy, and it is a direct result of the worldwide mobilization against them. To put the matter bluntly: we destroyed it – or at least, the IMF in anything like it's familiar form.[3] The World Bank is not doing all that much better. But by the time the full effects were felt, we weren't even paying attention.

This last story is worth telling in some detail, so let me leave the indented section here for a moment and continue in the main text:

3   This essay was written in 2007. The IMF still exists at this time of course (2011) but it's role has transformed almost completely and is internally much contested; though there has been an attempt to revive some of its old "structural adjustment" style approaches, this time within the European Union, these are meeting very strong resistance.

The IMF was always the arch-villain of the struggle. It is the most powerful, most arrogant, most pitiless instrument through which neoliberal policies have, for the last 25 years been imposed on the poorer countries of the global South, basically, by manipulating debt. In exchange for emergency refinancing, the IMF would demand "structural adjustment programs" that forced massive cuts in health, education, price supports on food, and endless privatization schemes that allowed foreign capitalists to buy up local resources at firesale prices. Structural adjustment never somehow worked to get countries back on their feet economically, but that just meant they remained in crisis, and the solution was always to insist on yet another round of structural adjustment.

The IMF had another, less celebrated, role: that of global enforcer. It was its job to ensure that no country (no matter how poor) could ever be allowed to default on loans to Western bankers (no matter how foolhardy). Imagine a banker were to offer a corrupt dictator a billion dollar loan, and that dictator placed it directly in his Swiss bank account and fled the country; the IMF's job was to ensure that, rather than be forgiven or renegotiated, let alone hunted down, that billion would still have to be extracted (plus generous interest) from the dictator's former victims. Under no conditions should Chase or Citibank have to take a loss. If a country did default, for any reason, the IMF could impose a credit boycott whose economic effects were roughly comparable to that of a nuclear bomb. (I note in passing that all this flies in the face of even elementary economic theory, whereby those lending money are supposed to be accepting a certain degree of risk; since it's only the danger of default that forces them to allocate money to productive investments. But in the world of international politics, economic laws are only held to be binding on the poor.) This role was their downfall.

What happened was that in 2002, Argentina defaulted and got away with it.

In the '90s, Argentina had been the IMF's star pupil in Latin America – they had literally privatized every public facility except the customs bureau. Then in 2001, the economy crashed. The immediate results we all know: battles in the streets, the creation of popular assemblies to run urban neighborhoods, the overthrow of three governments in one month, road blockades, occupied factories... "Horizontalism" – broadly anarchist, or at least anti-authoritarian principles – were at the core of popular resistance. Within a matter of months, political class was so completely discredited that politicians were obliged to put on wigs and phony mustaches to be able to eat in restaurants without being physically attacked. When Nestor Kirchner, a moderate social democrat, took power in 2003, he knew he had to do something dramatic in order to get most of the population even to accept even the idea of having a government, let alone his own. So he did. He did, in fact, the one thing no one in that position is ever supposed to do. He announced he simply wasn't going to play the bulk of Argentina's foreign debt.

Actually Kirchner was quite clever about it. He did not default on his IMF loans. He focused on Argentina's private debt, announcing that he was unilaterally writing them down by 75 cents on the dollar. The result was the greatest default in financial history. Citibank and Chase appealed to the IMF, their accustomed enforcer, to apply the usual punishment. But for the first time in its history, the IMF balked. First of all, with Argentina's economy already in ruins, even the economic equivalent of a nuclear bomb would do little more than make the rubble bounce. Second of all, just about everyone was aware it was the IMF's disastrous advice that set the stage for Argentina's crash in the first place. Third and most decisively, this was at the very height of the impact of the global justice movement: the IMF was already the most hated institution on the planet, and willfully destroying what little remained of the Argentine middle class would have been pushing things just a little bit too far.

So Argentina was allowed to get away with it. After that, everything was different. Before long, Brazil and Argentina together arranged to pay back their outstanding debt to the IMF itself as well. With a little help from Chavez, so did the rest of the continent. In 2003, Latin American IMF debt stood at $49 billion. Now it's $694 million.[4] To put that in perspective: that's a decline of 98.6%. For every thousand dollars owed four years ago, Latin America now owes fourteen bucks. Asia followed. China and India now both have no outstanding debt to the IMF and refuse to take out new loans. The boycott now includes Korea, Thailand, Indonesia, Malaysia, the Philippines and pretty much every other significant regional economy. Also Russia. The Fund is reduced to lording it

4   The essay was written in 2007.

over the economies of Africa, and maybe some parts of the Middle East and former Soviet sphere (basically those without oil). As a result its revenues have plummeted by 80% in four years. In the irony of all possible ironies, it's increasingly looking like the IMF will go bankrupt if they can't find someone willing to bail them out. Neither is it clear there's anyone particularly wants to. With its reputation as fiscal enforcer in tatters, the IMF no longer serves any obvious purpose even for capitalists. There's been a number of proposals at recent G8 meetings to make up a new mission for the organization – a kind of international bankruptcy court, perhaps – but all ended up getting torpedoed for one reason or another. Even if the IMF does survive, it has already been reduced to a cardboard cut-out of its former self.

The World Bank, which early on took on the role of good cop, is in somewhat better shape. But emphasis here must be placed on the word "somewhat" – as in, its revenue has only fallen by 60%, not 80%, and there are few actual boycotts. On the other hand the Bank is currently being kept alive largely by the fact India and China are still willing to deal with it, and both sides know that, so it is no longer in much of a position to dictate terms.

Obviously, all of this does not mean all the monsters have been slain. In Latin America, neoliberalism might be on the run, but China and India are carrying out devastating "reforms" within their own countries, European social protections are under attack, and most of Africa, despite much hypocritical posturing on the part of the Bonos and rich countries of the world, is still locked in debt, even as it faces a new colonization by China. The US, its economic power retreating in most of the world, is frantically trying to redouble its grip over Mexico and Central America. We're not living in utopia. But we already knew that. The question is why we never noticed the victories we *did* win.

Olivier de Marcellus, a PGA activist from Switzerland, points to one reason: whenever some element of the capitalist system takes a hit, whether it's the nuclear industry or the IMF, some leftist journal will start explaining to us that really, this is all part of their plan – or maybe, an effect of the inexorable working out of the internal contradictions of capital, but certainly, nothing for which we ourselves are in any way responsible. Even more important, perhaps, is our reluctance to even say the word "we." The Argentine default, wasn't that really engineered by Nestor Kirchner? He was

a politician! What does he have to do with anarchists or the globalization movement? I mean, it's not as if his hands were forced
by thousands of citizens were rising up, smashing banks, and replacing the government with popular assemblies coordinated by
the IMC! Or, well, okay, maybe it was. Well, in that case, those
citizens were People of Color in the Global South. How can "we"
take responsibility for their actions? Never mind that they mostly
saw themselves as part of the same global justice movement as us,
espoused similar ideas, wore similar clothes, used similar tactics,
in many cases even belonged to the same confederacies or organizations. Saying "we" here would imply the primal sin of speaking
for others.

Myself, I think it's reasonable for a global movement to consider its accomplishments in global terms. These are not incon-
siderable. Yet just as with the anti-nuclear movement, they were
almost all focused on the middle term. Let me map out a similar
hierarchy of goals:

1) **Short-Term Goals**: blockade and shut down particular
summit meetings (IMF, WTO, G8, etc)

2) **Medium-Term Goals**: destroy the "Washington
Consensus" around neoliberalism, block all new trade
pacts, delegitimize and ultimately shut down institutions
like the WTO, IMF, and World Bank; disseminate new
models of direct democracy.

3) **Long-Term Goals**: (at least for the more radical elements)
smash the state and destroy capitalism.

Here again, we find the same pattern. After the miracle of Seattle,
where activists actually did shut down the meetings, short term
– tactical – goals were rarely achieved. But this was mainly because faced with such a movement, governments tend to dig in
their heels and make it a matter of principle that they shouldn't
be. This was usually considered much more important, in fact,
than the success of the summit in question. Most activists do not
seem to be aware that in a lot of cases – the 2001 and 2002 IMF
and World Bank meetings for example – police ended up enforcing security arrangements so elaborate that they came very

close to shutting down the meetings themselves; ensuring that many events were cancelled, the ceremonies were ruined, and most delegates didn't really had a chance to talk to one other. But for the cops, the point was clearly not whether trade officials got to meet or not. The point was that the protestors could not be seen to win.

Here, too, the medium term goals were achieved so quickly that it actually made the longer-term goals more difficult. NGOs, labor unions, authoritarian Marxists, and similar allies jumped ship almost immediately; strategic debates ensued, but they were carried out, as always, indirectly, as arguments about race, privilege, tactics, almost anything but as actual strategic debates. Here, too, everything was made infinitely more difficult by the state's recourse to war.

It is hard, as I mentioned, for anarchists to take much direct responsibility for the inevitable end of the war in Iraq, or even to the very bloody nose the empire has already acquired there. But a case could well be made for indirect responsibility. Since the '60s, and the catastrophe of Vietnam, the US government has not abandoned its policy of answering any threat of democratic mass mobilizing by a return to war. But it has to be much more careful. Essentially, they now feel they have to design wars to be protest-proof. There is very good reason to believe that the first Gulf War, in 1991, was explicitly designed with this in mind. The approach taken to the invasion of Iraq – the insistence on a smaller, high-tech army, the extreme reliance on indiscriminate firepower, even against civilians, to protect against any Vietnam-like levels of American casualties – appears to have been developed, again, more with a mind to heading off any potential peace movement at home than one focused on military effectiveness. This, anyway, would help explain why the most powerful army in the world has ended up being tied down and even, periodically, defeated by an almost unimaginably ragtag group of guerillas with negligible access to outside safe-areas, funding, or military support – that is, until they resorted to a desperate combination of death squads, ethnic cleansing, massive bribery, and effectively turning over the country to their arch-enemy Iran. As in the trade summits, they are so obsessed with ensuring forces of civil resistance cannot be seen to win the battle at home that they would prefer to lose the actual war.

PERSPECTIVES (WITH A BRIEF RETURN TO '30s SPAIN)

How, then, to cope with the perils of victory? I can't claim to have any simple answers. Really I wrote this essay more to open up a conversation, to put the problem on the table – to inspire a strategic debate.

Still, some implications are pretty obvious. The next time we plan a major action campaign, I think we would do well to at least take into account the possibility that we might win. Or at least, that we might obtain our mid-range strategic goals very quickly, and that when that happens, many of our allies will fall away. We have to recognize strategic debates for what they are, even when they appear to be about something else. Take one famous example: arguments about property destruction after Seattle. Most of these, I think, were really arguments about capitalism. Those who decried window-breaking did so mainly because they wished to appeal to middle-class consumers to move towards global exchange-style green consumerism, and to ally with labor bureaucracies and social democrats abroad. This was not a path designed to provoke a direct confrontation with capitalism, and most of those who urged us to take this route were at least skeptical about the possibility that capitalism could ever really be defeated. Many were in fact in favor of capitalism, if in a significantly humanized form. Those who did break windows, on the other hand, didn't care if they offended suburban homeowners, because they did not figure that suburban homeowners were likely to ever become a significant element in any future revolutionary anticapitalist coalition. They were trying, in effect, to hijack the media to send a message that the system was vulnerable – hoping to inspire similar insurrectionary acts on the part of those who might considering entering a genuinely revolutionary alliance; alienated teenagers, oppressed people of color, undocumented workers, rank-and-file laborers impatient with union bureaucrats, the homeless, the unemployed, the criminalized, the radically discontent. If a militant anticapitalist movement was to begin, in America, it would have to start with people like these: people who don't need to be convinced that the system is rotten, only, that there's something they can do about it. And at any rate, even if it were possible to have an anticapitalist revolution without gun-battles in the streets – which most of us are hoping it is, since let's face it, if we come up against the US army, we will lose – there's no possible way we could have an

anticapitalist revolution while at the same time scrupulously re-
specting property rights. Yes, that will probably mean the suburban middle class will be the last to come on board. But they would
probably be the last to come on board anyway.[5]

The latter actually leads to an interesting question. What would
it mean to win, not just our medium-term goals, but our long term
ones? At the moment no one is even clear how that would come
about, for the very reason none of us have much faith remaining
in "the" revolution in the old 19th or 20th century sense of the
term. After all, the total view of revolution, that there will be a
single mass insurrection or general strike and then all walls will
come tumbling down, is entirely premised on the old fantasy of
capturing the state. That's the only way victory could possibly be
that absolute and complete – at least, if we are speaking of a whole
country or meaningful territory.

In way of illustration, consider this: What would it have actually meant for the Spanish anarchists to have actually "won" in
1937? It's amazing how rarely we ask ourselves such questions.
We just imagine it would have been something like the Russian
Revolution, which began in a similar way, with the melting away
of the old army, the spontaneous creation of workers' soviets.
But that was in the major cities. The Russian Revolution was
followed by years of civil war in which the Red Army gradually
imposed a new government's control on every part of the old
Russian Empire, whether the communities in question wanted it
or not. Let us imagine that anarchist militias in Spain had routed
the fascist army, and that army had completely dissolved. Let
us further imagine that it had successfully kicked the socialist Republican Government out of its offices in Barcelona and
Madrid. That would certainly have been anarchist victory by any-
body's standards. But what would have happened next? Would
they have established the entire territory of what had once been
Spain as a non-Republic, an anti-state existing within the exact
same international borders? Would they have imposed a regime
of popular councils in every singe village and municipality in the
territory of what had formerly been Spain? How? We have to
bear in mind here that were there were many villages, towns,
even regions of Spain where anarchists were few to non-existent.

---

5   And this probably remains true, no matter how deep their mortgages
    are under water.

In some, just about the entire population was made up of conservative Catholics or monarchists; in others (say, the Basque country) there was a militant and well-organized working class, but it that was overwhelmingly socialist or communist. Even at the height of revolutionary fervor, a significant portion of these would presumably stay true to their old values and ideas. If the victorious FAI attempted to exterminate them all – a task which would have required killing millions of people – or chase them out of the country, or forcibly relocate them into anarchist communities, or send them off to reeducation camps – they would not only have been guilty of world-class atrocities, they would also have had to give up on being anarchists. Democratic organizations simply cannot commit atrocities on that systematic scale: for that, you'd need Communist or Fascist-style top-down organization. This is because, as history has shown, while humans can be extraordinarily cruel in brief moments of extreme excitement, real atrocities take time: you can't actually get thousands of human beings to systematically massacre hundreds of thousands of helpless women, children and old people, destroy communities, or chase families from their ancestral homes – projects which take a considerable amount of methodical planning – unless they can at least tell themselves that someone else is responsible and they are only following orders.

As a result, there appear to have been only two possible solutions to the problem.

1) Allow the Spanish Republic to continue as de facto government under the socialists, perhaps with a few anarchist ministers (as did in fact exist during the war), allow them impose government control on the right-wing majority areas, and then get some kind of deal out of them that they would allow the anarchist-majority cities, towns, and villages to organize themselves as they wish to. Then hope that they kept the deal (this might be considered the "good luck" option)

2) Declare that everyone was to form their own local popular assemblies, and let each assembly decide on their own mode of self-organization.

The latter seems the more fitting with anarchist principles, but the results wouldn't have likely been too much different. After all, if the inhabitants of, say, Bilbao overwhelmingly desired to create a local government, with a mayor and police, how exactly would anarchists in Madrid or Barcelona have stopped them? Municipalities where the church or landlords still commanded popular support would presumably have put the same old right-wing authorities in charge; socialist or communist municipalities would have put socialist or communist party politicians and bureaucrats in charge; Right and Left statists would then each form rival confederations that, even though they controlled only a fraction of the former Spanish territory, would each declare themselves the legitimate government of Spain. Foreign governments would have recognized one or the other of the two confederations, depending on their own political leanings – since none would be willing to exchange ambassadors with a non-government like the FAI, even assuming the FAI wished to exchange ambassadors with them, which it wouldn't. In other words the actual shooting war might end, but the political struggle would continue, and large parts of Spain would presumably end up looking like contemporary Chiapas, with each district or community divided between anarchist and anti-anarchist factions. Ultimate victory would have had to be a long and arduous process. The only way to really win over the statist enclaves would be to win over their children, which could be accomplished by creating an obviously freer, more pleasurable, more beautiful, secure, relaxed, fulfilling life in the stateless sections. Foreign capitalist powers, on the other hand, even if they did not intervene militarily, would do everything possible to head off the notorious "threat of a good example" by economic boycotts and subversion, and pouring resources into the statist zones. In the end, everything would probably depend on the degree to which anarchist victories in Spain inspired similar insurrections elsewhere.

The real point of this imaginative exercise is just to point out that there are no clean breaks in history. The flip-side of the old idea of the clean break, the one moment when the state falls and capitalism is defeated, is that anything short of that is not really a victory at all. Revolutionaries hear this line continually. If capitalism is left standing, if it begins to market revolutionaries' once-subversive ideas, it shows that the capitalists really won. The revolutionaries have lost; they've been coopted. To me this entire line of reasoning is absurd. Feminism was surely a revolutionary force: what could be more radical than reversing thousands of years of gender oppressing lying at the very heart of what we think we are and can be and should be as human beings? Can we say that feminism lost, that it achieved nothing, just because corporate culture felt obliged to pay lip service to condemning sexism and capitalist firms began marketing feminist books, movies, and other products? Of course not. Unless you've managed to destroy capitalism and patriarchy in one fell blow, this is one of the clearest signs that you've gotten somewhere. Presumably any effective road to revolution will involve endless moments of cooptation, endless victorious campaigns, endless little insurrectionary moments or moments of flight and covert autonomy. I hesitate to even speculate what it might really be like. But to start in that direction, the first thing we need to do is to recognize that we do, in fact, win some. Actually, recently, we've been winning quite a lot. The question is how to break the cycle of exaltation and despair and come up with some strategic visions (the more the merrier) about these victories build on each other, to create a cumulative movement towards a new society.

Hope in Common

WE SEEM TO HAVE REACHED AN IMPASSE. CAPITALISM AS WE know it appears to be coming apart. But as financial institutions stagger and crumble, there is no obvious alternative. Organized resistance appears scattered and incoherent; the global justice movement a shadow of its former self. There is good reason to believe that, in a generation or so, capitalism will no longer exist: for the simple reason that (as many have pointed out) it's impossible to maintain an engine of perpetual growth forever on a finite planet. Yet faced with this prospect, the knee-jerk reaction – even of "progressives" and many ostensible anticapitalists – is, often, fear, to cling to what exists because they simply can't imagine an alternative that wouldn't be even more oppressive and destructive.

The first question we should be asking is: How did this happen? Is it normal for human beings to be unable to imagine what a better world would even be like?

Hopelessness isn't natural. It needs to be produced. If we really want to understand this situation, we have to begin by understanding that the last thirty years have seen the construction of a vast bureaucratic apparatus for the creation and maintenance of hopelessness, a kind of giant machine that is designed, first and foremost, to destroy any sense of possible alternative futures. At root is a veritable obsession on the part of the rulers of the world with ensuring that social movements cannot be seen to grow, to flourish, to propose alternatives; that those who challenge existing power arrangements can never, under any circumstances, be perceived to win. To do so requires creating a vast apparatus of armies, prisons, police, various forms of private security firms and police and military intelligence apparatus, propaganda engines of every conceivable variety, most of which do not attack alternatives directly so much as they create a pervasive climate of fear, jingoistic conformity, and simple despair that renders any thought of changing the world seem an idle fantasy. Maintaining this apparatus seems even more important, to exponents of the "free market," even than maintaining any sort of viable market economy. How else can one explain, for instance, what happened in the former Soviet Union, where one would have imagined the end of the Cold War would have led to the dismantling of the army and KGB and rebuilding the factories, but in fact what happened was precisely the other way around? This is just one extreme example of what has been happening everywhere. Economically, this apparatus is pure dead weight; all the guns, surveillance cameras, and propaganda engines are extraordinarily expensive and really produce nothing, and as a result, it's dragging the entire capitalist system down with it, and possibly, the earth itself.

The spirals of financialization and endless string of economic bubbles we've been experience are a direct result of this apparatus. It's no coincidence that the United States has become both the world's major military ("security") power and the major promoter of bogus securities. This apparatus exists to shred and pulverize the human imagination, to destroy any possibility of envisioning alternative futures. As a result, the only thing left to imagine is more and more money, and debt spirals entirely out of control. What is debt, after all, but imaginary money whose value can only be realized in the future: future profits, the proceeds of the exploitation of workers not yet born. Finance capital in turn is the buying and selling of these imaginary future profits; and once one assumes that capitalism itself will be around for all eternity, the only kind of economic democracy left to imagine is one everyone is equally free to invest in the market – to grab their own piece in the game of buying and selling imaginary future profits, even if these profits are to be extracted from themselves. Freedom has become the right to share in the proceeds of one's own permanent enslavement.

And since the bubble had built on the destruction of futures, once it collapsed there appeared to be – at least for the moment – simply nothing left.

The effect however is clearly temporary. If the story of the global justice movement tells us anything it's that the moment there appears to be any sense of an opening, the imagination will immediately spring forth. This is what effectively happened in the late '90s when it looked, for a moment, like we might be moving toward a world at peace. In the US, for the last fifty years, whenever there seems to be any possibility of peace breaking out, the same thing happens: the emergence of a radical social movement dedicated to principles of direct action and participatory democracy, aiming to revolutionize the very meaning of political life. In the late '50s it was the civil rights movement; in the late '70s, the anti-nuclear movement. This time it happened on a planetary scale, and challenged capitalism head-on. These movements tend to be extraordinarily effective. Certainly the global justice movement was. Few realize that one of the main reasons it seemed to flicker in and out of existence so rapidly was that it achieved its principle goals so quickly. None of us dreamed, when we were organizing the protests in Seattle in 1999 or at the IMF meetings in DC in 2000, that within a mere three or four years, the WTO process would have collapsed, that "free trade" ideologies would be considered almost entirely discredited, that every new trade pact they threw at us – from the MIA to Free Trade Areas of the Americas act – would have been defeated, the World Bank hobbled, the power of the IMF over most of the world's population, effectively destroyed. But this is precisely what happened. The fate of the IMF is particularly startling. Once the terror of the Global South, it is, by now, a shattered remnant of its former self, reviled and discredited, reduced to selling off its gold reserves and desperately searching for a new global mission. Meanwhile, most of the "third world debt" has simply vanished. All of this was a direct result of a movement that managed to mobilize global resistance so effectively that the reigning institutions were first discredited, and ultimately, that those running governments in Asia and especially Latin America were forced by their own populations to call the bluff of the international financial system. As I have already argued, much of the reason the movement was thrown into confusion was because none of us had really considered we might win.

But of course there's another reason. Nothing terrifies the rulers of the world, and particularly of the United States, as much as the danger of grassroots democracy. Whenever a genuinely democratic movement begins to emerge – particularly, one based on principles of civil disobedience and direct action – the reaction is the same; the government makes immediate concessions (fine, you can have voting rights; no nukes), then starts ratcheting up military tensions abroad. The movement is then forced to transform itself into an anti-war movement; which, pretty much invariably, is far less democratically organized. So the civil rights movement was followed by Vietnam, the anti-nuclear movement by proxy wars in El Salvador and Nicaragua, the global justice movement, by the "War on Terror." But at this point, we can see that "war" for what it was: as the flailing and obviously doomed effort of a declining power to make its peculiar combination of bureaucratic war machines and speculative financial capitalism into a permanent global condition. If the rotten architecture collapsed abruptly at the end of 2008, it was at least in part because so much of the work had already been accomplished by a movement that had, in the face of the surge of repression after 9/11, combined with confusion over how to follow up its startling initial success, had seemed to have largely disappeared from the scene.

Of course it hasn't really.

We are clearly at the verge of another mass resurgence of the popular imagination. It's just a matter of time. Certainly, the first reaction to an unforeseen crisis is usually shock and confusion; but after a bit, that passes, and new ideas emerge. It shouldn't be that difficult. Most of the elements are already there. For the moment the problem is that, our perceptions having been twisted into knots by decades of relentless propaganda, we are no longer able to see them. Consider here the term "communism." Rarely has a term come to be so utterly reviled. The standard line, which we accept more or less unthinkingly, is that communism means state control of the economy, and this is an impossible utopian dream because history has shown it simply "doesn't work." Capitalism, however unpleasant, is therefore the only remaining option.

All this is based on identifying "communism" with the sort of system that existed in the old Soviet bloc, or China – a top-down command economy. Granted, under some circumstances, particularly when playing industrial catch-up, organizing vast projects like space programs, or especially, fighting wars, these systems can be surprisingly efficient. This is why the capitalist powers were so frightened in the '30s: the Soviet Union was growing at 10% a year even as everyone else was stagnating. But the irony is that the people who organized these systems, even though they called themselves Communists, never claimed that this top-down system itself was "communism." They called it "socialism" (another arguable point, but we'll leave that one aside for a moment), and saw communism as a utopian truly free, stateless society that would exist at some point in the unknowable future. Granted, the system they did create deserves to be reviled. But it has almost nothing to do with communism in the original sense of the term.

In fact communism really just means any situation where people act according to the principle of "from each according to their abilities, to each according to their needs" – which is the way pretty much everyone always act if they are working together to get something done. If two people are fixing a pipe and one says "hand me the wrench," the other doesn't say, "and what do I get for it?"(That is, if they actually want it to be fixed.) This is true even if they happen to be employed by Bechtel or Citigroup. They apply principles of communism because it's the only thing that really works. This is also the reason whole cities or countries so often revert to some form of rough-and-ready communism in the wake of natural disasters, or economic collapse (one might say, in those circumstances, markets and hierarchical chains of command are luxuries they can't afford.) The more creativity is required, the more people have to improvise at a given task, the more egalitarian the resulting form of communism is likely to be: that's why even Republican computer engineers, when trying to innovate new software ideas, tend to form small democratic collectives. It's only when work becomes standardized and boring – as on production lines – that it becomes possible to impose more authoritarian, even fascistic forms of communism. But the fact is that even private companies are, internally, organized communistically – even if that communism often takes extraordinarily unpleasant forms.

Communism, then, is already here. The question is how to further democratize it. Capitalism, in turn, is just one possible way of managing communism – and, it has become increasingly clear, rather a disastrous one. Clearly we need to be thinking about a better one: preferably, one that does not set us all quite so systematically at each others' throats.

All this makes it much easier to understand why capitalists are willing to pour such extraordinary resources into the machinery of hopelessness. Capitalism is not just a poor system for managing communism: it has a notorious tendency to periodically come spinning apart. Each time it does, those who profit from it have to convince everyone – and most of all the technical people, the doctors and teachers and surveyors and insurance claims adjustors – that there is really no choice but to dutifully paste it all back together again, in something like the original form. This despite the fact that most of those who will end up doing the work of rebuilding the system don't even like it very much, and all have at least the vague suspicion, rooted in their own innumerable experiences of everyday communism, that it really ought to be possible to create a system at least a little less stupid and unfair.

This is why, as the Great Depression showed, the existence of *any* plausible-seeming alternative – even one so dubious as the Soviet Union of the 1930s – can, as Massimo de Angelis points out – turn a mere downswing of capitalist boom-bust cycle into an apparently insoluble political crisis.

This in turn helps explain the weird ideological contortions by which we are constantly told "communism just doesn't work." I have seen mothers tell this to their twelve-year-old daughters when they so much as suggest sharing tasks cooperatively. (As if the problem with the Soviet Union was that they didn't have anyone giving orders!) In fact, it's downright bizarre to observe how quickly the standard rhetoric went from saying that a system like the Soviet Union, with no internal market would not possibly compete either technologically or in the provision of consumer goods with their richest and most advanced capitalist rivals, to saying that such a society could not exist at all. Actually, I might remind my readers, it did. For over eighty years. It was a world power, defeated Hitler, and shot astronauts into outer space. I should emphasize that no one in their right mind would ever wish to recreate such a system. But the ideological work of pretending it was somehow impossible seems designed, really, to convincing us that *real* communism, real everyday communism, of the sort the Soviet Union and its allies never actually embraced, cannot possibly be of any larger social significance. Because if start thinking about the way our lives really work, we might not be so eager to continue obeying orders, and dutifully rebuild the apparatus of our own oppression whenever it breaks down again.

Not that anyone in their right mind would ever dream of recreating something like the old Soviet Union. Those wishing to subvert the system have mostly learned by now, from bitter experience, that we cannot place our faith in states of any kind. In some parts of the world, governments and their representatives have largely pulled up stakes and left: there are whole swathes of Africa and Southeast Asia, and probably parts of the Americas, where the presence of state and capital is minimal, or even non-existent, but since people have shown no inclination to kill one another, no one has really noticed. Some of these have been improvising new social arrangements we simply have no way to know about. In others, the last decade has seen the development of thousands of forms of mutual aid association in open defiance of states and capital, most of which have not even made it onto the radar of the global media. They range from tiny cooperatives and associations to vast anticapitalist experiments, archipelagos of occupied factories in Paraguay or Argentina or of self-organized tea plantations and fisheries in India, autonomous institutes in Korea, whole insurgent communities in Chiapas or Bolivia, associations of landless peasants, urban squatters, neighborhood alliances, that spring up pretty much anywhere that where state power and global capital seem to temporarily looking the other way. All these experiments may have almost no ideological unity and most are not even aware of the other's existence, but all are marked by a common desire to break with the logic of capital. And in many places, they are beginning to combine. "Economies of solidarity" exist on every continent, in at least eighty different countries. We are at the point where we can begin to perceive the outlines of how these can knit together on a global level, creating new forms of planetary commons to create a genuine insurgent civilization.

Visible alternatives shatter the sense of inevitability, that the system must, necessarily, be patched together in the same form – this is why it became such an imperative of global governance to stamp them out, or, when that's not possible, to ensure that no one knows about them. To become aware of it allows us to see everything we are already doing in a new light. To realize we're all already communists when working on a common projects, all already anarchists when we solve problems without recourse to lawyers or police, all revolutionaries when we make something genuinely new.

One might object: a revolution cannot confine itself to this. That's true. In this respect, the great strategic debates are really just beginning. I'll offer one suggestion though. For at least five thousand years, popular movements have tended to center on struggles over debt – this was true long before capitalism even existed. There is a reason for this. Debt is the most efficient means ever created to take relations that are fundamentally based on violence and violent inequality and to make them seem right and moral to everyone concerned. When the trick no longer works, everything explodes. As it is now. Clearly, debt has shown itself to be the point of greatest weakness of the system, the point where it spirals out of anyone's control. It also allows endless opportunities for organizing. Some speak of a debtor's strike, or debtor's cartel. Perhaps so – but at the very least we can start with a pledge against evictions: to pledge, neighborhood by neighborhood, to support each other if any of us are to be driven from our homes. The power is not just that to challenge regimes of debt is to challenge the very fiber of capitalism – its moral foundation – now revealed to be a collection of broken promises – but in doing so, to create a new one. A debt after all is only that: a promise, and the present world abounds with promises that have not been kept. One might speak here of the promise made us by the state; that if we abandon any right to collectively manage our own affairs, we would at least be provided with basic life security. Or of the promise offered by capitalism – that we could live like kings if we were willing to buy stock in our own collective subordination. All of this has come crashing down. What remains is what we are able to promise one another. Directly. Without the mediation of economic and political bureaucracies. The revolution begins by asking: what sort of promises do free men and women make to one another, and how, by making them, do we begin to make another world?

Revolution in Reverse

"ALL POWER TO THE IMAGINATION." "BE REALISTIC, DEMAND the impossible..." Anyone involved in radical politics has heard these expressions a thousand times. Usually they charm and excite the first time one encounters them, then eventually become so familiar as to seem hackneyed, or just disappear into the ambient background noise of radical life. Rarely if ever are they the object of serious theoretical reflection.

It seems to me that at the current historical juncture, some such reflection wouldn't be a bad idea. We are at a moment, after all, when received definitions have been thrown into disarray. It is quite possible that we are heading for a revolutionary moment, or perhaps a series of them, but we no longer have any clear idea of what that might even mean. This essay then is the product of a sustained effort to try to rethink terms like realism, imagination, alienation, bureaucracy, and revolution itself. It's born of some six years of involvement with the alternative globalization movement and particularly with its most radical, anarchist, direct action-oriented elements. Consider it a kind of preliminary theoretical report. I want to ask, among other things, why is it these terms, which for most of us seem rather to evoke long-since forgotten debates of the 1960s, still resonate in those circles? Why is it that the idea of any radical social transformation so often seems "unrealistic"? What does revolution mean once one no longer expects a single, cataclysmic break with past structures of oppression? These seem disparate questions but it seems to me the answers are related. If in many cases I brush past existing bodies of theory, this is quite intentional: I am trying to see if it is possible to build on the experience of these movements and the theoretical currents that inform them to begin to create something new.

Here is gist of my argument:

1) Right and Left political perspectives are founded, above all, on different assumptions about the ultimate realities of power. The Right is rooted in a political ontology of violence, where being realistic means taking into account the forces of destruction. In reply the Left has consistently proposed variations on a political ontology of the imagination, in which the forces that are seen as the ultimate realities that need to be taken into account are those (forces of production, creativity...) that bring things into being.

2) The situation is complicated by the fact that systematic inequalities backed by the threat of force – structural violence – always produce skewed and fractured structures of the imagination. It is the experience of living inside these fractured structures that we refer to as "alienation."

3) Our customary conception of revolution is insurrectionary: the idea is to brush aside existing realities of violence by overthrowing the state, then, to unleash the powers of popular imagination and creativity to overcome the structures that create alienation. Over the twentieth century it eventually became apparent that the real problem was how to institutionalize such creativity without creating new, often even more violent and alienating structures. As a result, the insurrectionary model no longer seems completely viable, but it's not clear what will replace it.

4) One response has been the revival of the tradition of direct action. In practice, mass actions reverse the ordinary insurrectionary sequence. Rather than a dramatic

confrontation with state power leading first to an outpouring of popular festivity, the creation of new democratic institutions, and eventually the reinvention of everyday life, in organizing mass mobilizations, activists
drawn principally from subcultural groups create new,
directly democratic institutions to organize "festivals of
resistance" that ultimately lead to confrontations with the
state. This is just one aspect of a more general movement
of reformulation that seems to me to be inspired in part
by the influence of anarchism, but in even larger part, by
feminism – a movement that ultimately aims recreate the
effects of those insurrectionary moments on an ongoing
basis

Let me take these one by one.

Part I: "be realistic..."

FROM EARLY 2000 to late 2002 I was working with the Direct
Action Network in New York – the principal group responsible
for organizing mass actions as part of the global justice movement in that city at that time. Actually, DAN was not, technical-
ly, a group, but a decentralized network, operating on principles
of direct democracy according to an elaborate, but strikingly
effective, form of consensus process. It played a central role in
ongoing efforts to create new organizational forms that I wrote
about in an earlier essay in these pages. DAN existed in a purely
political space; it had no concrete resources, not even a significant treasury, to administer. Then one day someone gave DAN a
car. This caused a minor, but ongoing, crisis. We soon discovered
that legally, it is impossible for a decentralized network to own
a car. Cars can be owned by individuals, or they can be owned
by corporations, which are fictive individuals. Governments can
also own cars. But they cannot be owned by networks. Unless
we were willing to incorporate ourselves as a nonprofit corpora-
tion (which would have required a complete reorganization and
abandoning most of our egalitarian principles) the only expedi-
ent was to find a volunteer willing to claim to be the owner for
legal purposes. But then that person was held responsible for
all outstanding fines, insurance fees, and had to provide written

permission to allow anyone else to drive the car out of state; and, of course, only he could retrieve the car if it were impounded. Before long the DAN car had become such a perennial problem that we abandoned it.

It struck me there was something important here. Why is it that projects like DAN's – projects of democratizing society – are so often perceived as idle dreams that melt away as soon as they encounter hard material reality? In our case, at least, it had nothing to do with inefficiency: police chiefs across the country had called us the best organized force they'd ever had to deal with. It seems to me the reality effect (if one may call it that) comes rather from the fact that radical projects tend to founder, or at least become endlessly difficult, the moment they enter into the world of large, heavy objects: buildings, cars, tractors, boats, industrial machinery. This in turn is not because these objects are somehow intrinsically difficult to administer democratically – history is full of communities that succesfully engage in the democratic administration of common resources – it's because, like the DAN car, they are surrounded by endless government regulation, and effectively impossible to hide from the government's armed representatives. In America, I have seen endless examples of this dilemma. A squat is legalized after a long struggle; suddenly, building inspectors arrive to announce it will take ten thousand dollars worth of repairs to bring it up to code. Organizers are therefore forced spend the next several years organizing bake sales and soliciting contributions. This means setting up bank accounts, and legal regulations then specify how a group receiving funds, or dealing with the government, must be organized (again, *not* as an egalitarian collective). All these regulations are enforced by violence. True, in ordinary life, police rarely come in swinging billy clubs to enforce building code regulations, but, as anarchists often discover, if one simply pretends the state and its regulations don't exist, that will, eventually, happen. The rarity with which the nightsticks actually appear just helps to make the violence harder to see. This in turn makes the effects of all these regulations – regulations that almost always assume that normal relations between individuals are mediated by the market, and that normal groups are organized by relations of hierarchy and command – seem to emanate not from the government's monopoly of the use of force, but from the largeness, solidity, and heaviness of the objects themselves.

When one is asked to be "realistic" then, the reality one is normally being asked to recognize is not one of natural, material facts; neither is it really some supposed ugly truth about human nature. Normally it's a recognition of the effects of the systematic threat of violence. It even threads our language. Why, for example, is a building referred to as "real property," or "real estate"? The "real" in this usage is not derived from Latin *res*, or "thing": it's from the Spanish *real*, meaning, "royal," "belonging to the king." All land within a sovereign territory ultimately belongs to the sovereign; legally this is still the case. This is why the state has the right to impose its regulations. But sovereignty ultimately comes down to a monopoly of what is euphemistically referred to as "force" – that is, violence. Just as Giorgio Agamben famously argued that from the perspective of sovereign power, something is alive because you can kill it, so property is "real" because the state can seize or destroy it. In the same way, when one takes a "realist" position in International Relations, one assumes that states will use whatever capacities they have at their disposal, including force of arms, to pursue their national interests. What "reality" is one recognizing? Certainly not material reality. The idea that nations are human-like entities with purposes and interests is entirely metaphysical. The King of France had purposes and interests. "France" does not. What makes it seem "realistic" to suggest it does is simply that those in control of nation-states have the power to raise armies, launch invasions, bomb cities, and can otherwise threaten the use of organized violence in the name of what they describe as their "national interests" – and that it would be foolish to ignore that possibility. National interests are real because they can kill you.

The critical term here is "force," as in "the state's monopoly of the use of coercive force." Whenever we hear this word invoked, we find ourselves in the presence of a political ontology in which the power to destroy, to cause others pain or to threaten to break, damage, or mangle others bodies (or just lock them in a tiny room for the rest of their lives) is treated as the social equivalent of the very energy that drives the cosmos. Contemplate, if you will, the metaphors and displacements that make it possible to construct the following two sentences:

Scientists investigate the nature of physical laws so as to understand the forces that govern the universe.

> Police are experts in the scientific application of physical
> force in order to enforce the laws that govern society.

This is to my mind the essence of Right-wing thought: a political ontology that through such subtle means, allows violence to define the very parameters of social existence and common sense.

The Left, on the other hand, has always been founded on a different set of assumptions about what is ultimately real – about the very grounds of political being. Obviously Leftists don't deny the reality of violence. Many Leftist theorists think about it quite a lot. But they don't tend to give it the same foundational status.[1] Instead, I would argue that Leftist thought is founded on what I will call a "political ontology of the imagination" (I might just as easily have called it an ontology of creativity or making or invention.[2]) Nowadays, most of us tend to identify this tendency with the legacy of Marx, with his emphasis on social revolution and forces of material production. But even Marx was ultimately only a man of his time, and his terms emerged from much wider arguments about value, labor, and creativity current in radical circles of his day, whether in the worker's movement, or for that matter in various strains of Romanticism and bohemian life emerging around him in Paris and London at the time. Marx himself, for all his contempt for the utopian socialists of his day, never ceased to insist that what makes human beings different from animals is that architects, unlike bees, first raise their structures in the imagination. It was the unique property of humans, for Marx, that they first envision things, and only then bring them into being. It was this process he referred to as "production." Around the same time, utopian socialists like

---

1   Hence Mao might have written that "political power comes from the barrel of a gun" but he was also, as a Marxist, committed to the principle that structures and relations of economic production, rather than political power, is ultimately determinant of social reality.

2   Both perspectives are at the very least partial. The division itself, I would argue, is the product of certain peculiar features of Western theories of knowledge: particularly, the tendency to see the world not in terms of processes but as a collection a discrete, self-identical objects. We tend to hide away the creation and destruction of objects just as we do birth and death; the result is that "forces" of creation and destruction end up seeming the hidden reality behind everything.

St. Simon were arguing that artists needed to become the *avant garde* or "vanguard," as he put it, of a new social order, providing the grand visions that industry now had the power to bring into being. What at the time might have seemed the fantasy of an eccentric pamphleteer soon became the charter for a sporadic, uncertain, but apparently permanent alliance that endures to this day. If artistic avant gardes and social revolutionaries have felt a peculiar affinity for one another ever since, borrowing each other's languages and ideas, it appears to have been insofar as both have remained committed to the idea that the ultimate, hidden truth of the world is that it is something that we make, and, could just as easily make differently. In this sense, a phrase like "all power to the imagination" expresses the very quintessence of the Left.

To this emphasis on forces of creativity and production of course the Right tends to reply that revolutionaries systematically neglect the social and historical importance of the "means of destruction": states, armies, executioners, barbarian invasions, criminals, unruly mobs, and so on. Pretending such things are not there, or can simply be wished away, they argue, has the result of ensuring that left-wing regimes will in fact create far more death and destruction than those that have the wisdom to take a more "realistic" approach.

Obviously, the dichotomy I am proposing is very much a simplification. One could level endless qualifications. The bourgeoisie of Marx's time for instance had an extremely productivist philosophy – one reason Marx could see it as a revolutionary force. Elements of the Right dabbled with the artistic ideal, and 20th century Marxist regimes often embraced essentially right-wing theories of power, and paid little more than lip service to the determinant nature of production. Nonetheless, I think these are useful terms because even if one treats "imagination" and "violence" not as the single hidden truth of the world but as immanent principles, as equal constituents of any social reality, they can reveal a great deal one would not be able to see otherwise. For one thing, everywhere, imagination and violence seem to interact in predictable, and quite significant, ways.

Let me start with a few words on violence, providing a very schematic overview of arguments that I have developed in somewhat greater detail elsewhere:

Part II: on violence and imaginative displacement

I'M AN ANTHROPOLOGIST by profession and anthropological dis-
cussions of violence are almost always prefaced by statements that
violent acts are acts of communication, that they are inherently
meaningful, and that this is what is truly important about them.
In other words, violence operates largely through the imagination.

This is of course true. No reasonable person would discount the
importance of fear and terror in human life. Acts of violence can
be – indeed usually are – acts of communication of one sort or
another.[3] But the same could be said of any form of human action.
It strikes me that what is really important about violence is that it
is perhaps the only form of human action that holds out the possibility of operating on others *without* being communicative. Or
let me put this more precisely. Violence may well be the only way
in which it is possible for one human being to have relatively predictable effects on the actions of another without understanding
anything about them. Pretty much any other way one might try
to influence another's actions, one at least has to have some idea
who they think they are, who they think you are, what they might
want out of the situation, and a host of similar considerations. Hit
them over the head hard enough, all this becomes irrelevant. It's
true that the effects one can have by hitting them are quite limited.
But they are real enough, and the fact remains that any alternative form of action cannot, without some sort of appeal to shared
meanings or understandings, have any sort of effect at all. What's
more, even attempts to influence another by the threat of violence,
which clearly does require some level of shared understandings
(at the very least, the other party must understand they are being
threatened, and what is being demanded of them), requires much
less than any alternative. Most human relations – particularly ongoing ones, such as those between longstanding friends or longstanding enemies – are extremely complicated, endlessly dense
with experience and meaning. They require a continual and often
subtle work of interpretation; everyone involved must put constant energy into imagining the other's point of view. Threatening

---

3   This is of course all the more true when done by governments. A psy-
    chopath might torture and kill a victim and not wish anyone to know
    – though even they are prone to leave clues and monitor news stories.
    But when governments torture and kill people, the entire point is that
    others know they are doing it.

others with physical harm on the other hand allows the possibility of cutting through all this. It makes possible relations of a far more schematic kind: i.e., 'cross this line and I will shoot you and otherwise I really don't care who you are or what you want'. This is, for instance, why violence is so often the preferred weapon of the stupid: one could almost say, the trump card of the stupid, since it is that form of stupidity to which it is most difficult to come up with an intelligent response.

There is, however, one crucial qualification to be made here. The more evenly matched two parties are in their capacity for violence, the less all this tends to be true. If two parties are engaged in a relatively equal contest of violence, it is indeed a very good idea for each to understand as much as possible about the other. A military commander will obviously try to get inside his opponent's mind. Two duelists, or boxers, will try to anticipate the other's next move. It's really only when one side has an overwhelming advantage in their capacity to cause physical harm this is no longer the case. Of course, when one side has an overwhelming advantage, they rarely have to actually resort to actually shooting, beating, or blowing people up. The mere threat will usually suffice. This has a curious effect. It means that the most characteristic quality of violence – its capacity to impose very simple social relations that involve little or no imaginative identification – becomes most salient in situations defined by the possibility of violence, but where actual, physical violence is least likely to be present.

Ordinarily this is referred to as structural violence: all those systematic inequalities that are ultimately backed up by the threat of force, and therefore, can be seen as a form of violence in themselves. As feminists have long pointed out, systems of structural violence invariably seem to produce extreme lopsided structures of imaginative identification. It's not that interpretive work isn't carried out. Society, in any recognizable form, could not operate without it. Rather, the overwhelming burden of that interpretive labor is relegated to its victims.

Let me start with the patriarchal household. A constant staple of 1950s situation comedies, in America, were jokes about the impossibility of understanding women. The jokes of course were always told by men. Women's logic was always being treated as alien and incomprehensible. One never had the impression, on the other hand, that women had much trouble understanding the men. That's because the women had no choice but to understand men: since most women at the time had no access to their own income or resources, they had little choice but to spend a great deal of time and energy trying to understand what the important men in their lives thought was going on. Actually, this sort of rhetoric about the mysteries of womankind is a perennial feature of patriarchal families: structures that can, certainly, be considered forms of structural violence insofar as the power of men over women within them is, as generations of feminists have pointed out, ultimately backed up, if often in indirect and hidden ways, by all sorts of coercive force. But generations of female novelists – Virginia Wolfe comes immediately to mind – have also documented the other side of this: the constant work women perform in managing, maintaining, and adjusting the egos of apparently oblivious men – involving an endless work of imaginative identification and what I've called interpretive labor. This carries over on every level. Women are always imagining what things look like from a male point of view. Men almost never do the same for women.

This is presumably the reason why in so many societies with a pronounced gendered division of labor (that is, most societies), women know a great deal about men do every day, and men have next to no idea what women do. Faced with the prospect of even trying to imagine a women's daily life and general perspective on the world, many recoil in horror. In the US, one popular trick among high school creative writing teachers is to assign students to write an essay imagining that they were to switch genders, and describe what it would be like to live for one day as a member of the opposite sex. The results are almost always exactly the same: all the girls in class write long and detailed essays demonstrating that they have spent a great deal of time thinking about such questions; roughly half the boys refuse to write the essay entirely. Almost invariably they express profound resentment about having to imagine what it might be like to be a woman.

It should be easy enough to multiply parallel examples. When something goes wrong in a restaurant kitchen, and the boss appears to size things up, he is unlikely to pay much attention to a collection of workers all scrambling to explain their version of the story. Likely as not he'll tell them all to shut up and just arbitrarily decide what he thinks is likely to have happened: "you're the new guy, you must have messed up – if you do it again, you're fired."

It's those who do not have the power to fire arbitrarily who have to do the work of figuring out what actually happened. What occurs on the most petty or intimate level also occurs on the level of society as a whole. Curiously enough it was Adam Smith, in his *Theory of Moral Sentiments* (written in 1761), who first made notice of what's nowadays labeled "compassion fatigue." Human beings, he observed, appear to have a natural tendency not only to imaginatively identify with their fellows, but also, as a result, to actually feel one another's joys and pains. The poor, however, are just too consistently miserable, and as a result, observers, for their own self-protection, tend to simply blot them out. The result is that while those on the bottom spend a great deal of time imagining the perspectives of, and actually caring about, those on the top, but it almost never happens the other way around. That is my real point. Whatever the mechanisms, something like this always seems to occur: whether one is dealing with masters and servants, men and women, bosses and workers, rich and poor. Structural inequality – structural violence – invariably creates the same lopsided structures of the imagination. And since, as Smith correctly observed, imagination tends to bring with it sympathy, the victims of structural violence tend to care about its beneficiaries, or at least, to care far more about them than those beneficiaries care about them. In fact, this might well be (apart from the violence itself) the single most powerful force preserving such relations.[4]

It is easy to see bureaucratic procedures as an extension of this phenomenon. One might say they are not so much themselves forms of stupidity and ignorance as modes of organizing situations already marked by stupidity and ignorance owing the existence of structural violence. True, bureaucratic procedure operates as if it were a form of stupidity, in that it invariably means ignoring all the subtleties of real human existence and reducing everything to simple pre-established mechanical or statistical formulae. Whether it's a matter of forms, rules, statistics, or questionnaires, bureaucracy is always about simplification. Ultimately

---

4   While I am drawing on a broad range of feminist theory here, the most important is "standpoint theory": the key notes to consult here are Patricia Hill Collins, Donna Haraway, Sandra Harding, and Nancy Harstock. Some of the thoughts on imagination were originally inspired by observations by bell hooks about folk knowledge about white people in Southern African-American communities.

the effect is not so different than the boss who walks in to make an arbitrary snap decision as to what went wrong: it's a matter of applying very simple schemas to complex, ambiguous situations. The same goes, in fact, for police, who are after all simply low-level administrators with guns. Police sociologists have long since demonstrated that only a tiny fraction of police work has anything to do with crime. Police are, rather, the immediate representatives of the state's monopoly of violence, those who step in to actively simplify situations (for example, were someone to actively challenge some bureaucratic definition.) Simultaneously, police they have become, in contemporary industrial democracies, America in particular, the almost obsessive objects of popular imaginative identification. In fact, the public is constantly invited, in a thousand TV shows and movies, to see the world from a police officer's perspective, even if it is always the perspective of imaginary police officers, the kind who actually do spend their time fighting crime rather than concerning themselves with broken tail lights or open container laws.

IIa: excursus on transcendent versus immanent imagination

To IMAGINATIVELY IDENTIFY with an imaginary policeman is of course not the same as to imaginatively identify with a real policeman (most Americans in fact avoid real policeman like the plague). This is a critical distinction, however much an increasingly digitalized world makes it easy to confuse the two.

It is here helpful to consider the history of the word "imagination." The common Ancient and Medieval conception, what we call "the imagination" was considered the zone of passage between reality and reason. Perceptions from the material world had to pass through the imagination, becoming emotionally charged in the process and mixing with all sorts of phantasms, before the rational mind could grasp their significance. Intentions and desires moved in the opposite direction. It's only after Descartes, really, that the word "imaginary" came to mean, specifically, anything that is not real: imaginary creatures, imaginary places (Middle Earth, Narnia, planets in faraway Galaxies, the Kingdom of Prester John...), imaginary friends. By this definition of course a "political ontology of the imagination" would actually a contradiction in terms. The imagination cannot be the basis of reality. It is by definition that which we can think, but has no reality.

I'll refer to this latter as "the transcendent notion of the imagination" since it seems to take as its model novels or other works of fiction that create imaginary worlds that presumably, remain the same no matter how many times one reads them. Imaginary creatures – elves or unicorns or TV cops – are not affected by the real world. They cannot be, since they don't exist. In contrast, the kind of imagination I have been referring to here is much closer to the old, immanent, conception. Critically, it is in no sense static and free-floating, but entirely caught up in projects of action that aim to have real effects on the material world, and as such, always changing and adapting. This is equally true whether one is crafting a knife or a piece of jewelry, or trying to make sure one doesn't hurt a friend's feelings.

One might get a sense of how important this distinction really is by returning to the '68 slogan about giving power to the imagination. If one takes this to refer to the transcendent imagination – preformed utopian schemes, for example – doing so can, we know, have disastrous effects. Historically, it has often meant imposing them by violence. On the other hand, in a revolutionary situation, one might by the same token argue that *not* giving full power to the other, immanent, sort of imagination would be equally disastrous.

The relation of violence and imagination is made much more complicated because while structural inequalities always tend to split society into those doing imaginative labor, and those who do not, they can do so in very different ways. Capitalism here is a dramatic case in point. Political economy tend to see work in capitalist societies as divided between two spheres: wage labor, for which the paradigm is always factories, and domestic labor – housework, childcare – relegated mainly to women. The first is seen primarily as a matter of creating and maintaining physical objects. The second is probably best seen as a matter of creating and maintaining people and social relations. The distinction is obviously a bit of a caricature: there has never been a society, not even Engel's Manchester or Victor Hugo's Paris, where most men were factory workers or most women worked exclusively as housewives. Still, it is useful starting point, since it reveals an interesting divergence. In the sphere of industry, it is generally those on top that relegate to themselves the more imaginative tasks (i.e., that design the products and organize production),[5] whereas when inequalities emerge in the sphere of social production, it's those on the bottom who end up expected to the major imaginative work (for example, the bulk of what I've called the 'labor of interpretation' that keeps life running).

No doubt all this makes it easier to see the two as fundamentally different sorts of activity, making it hard for us to recognize interpretive labor, for example, or most of what we usually think of as women's work, as labor at all. To my mind it would probably be better to recognize it as the primary form of labor. Insofar as a clear distinction can be made here, it's the care, energy, and labor directed at human beings that should be considered fundamental. The things we care most about – our loves, passions, rivalries, obsessions – are always other people; and in most societies that are not capitalist, it's taken for granted that the manufacture of material goods is a subordinate moment in a larger process of fashioning people. In fact, I would argue that one of the most alienating aspects of capitalism is the fact that it forces us to pretend that it is the other way around, and that societies exist primarily to increase their output of things.

Part III: on alienation

> *In the twentieth century, death terrifies men less*
> *than the absence of real life. All these dead, mecha-*
> *nized, specialized actions, stealing a little bit of life*
> *a thousand times a day until the mind and body*
> *are exhausted, until that death which is not the*
> *end of life but the final saturation with absence.*
>
> *Raoul Vaneigem,*
> The Revolution of Everyday Life

CREATIVITY AND DESIRE – what we often reduce, in political economy terms, to "production" and "consumption" – are essentially vehicles of the imagination. Structures of inequality and domination, structural violence if you will, tend to skew the

5   It's not entirely clear to me how much this is a general pattern, or how much it is a peculiar feature of capitalism.

imagination. They might create situations where laborers are relegated to mind-numbing, boring, mechanical jobs and only a small elite is allowed to indulge in imaginative labor, leading to the feeling, on the part of the workers, that they are alienated from their own labor, that their very deeds belong to someone else. It might also create social situations where kings, politicians, celebrities or CEOs prance about oblivious to almost everything around them while their wives, servants, staff, and handlers spend all their time engaged in the imaginative work of maintaining them in their fantasies. Most situations of inequality I suspect combine elements of both.[6]

The subjective experience of living inside such lopsided structures of imagination is what we are referring to when we talk about "alienation."

It strikes me that if nothing else, this perspective would help explain the lingering appeal of theories of alienation in revolutionary circles, even when the academic Left has long since abandoned them. If one enters an anarchist infoshop, almost anywhere in the world, the French authors one is likely to encounter will still largely consist of Situationists like Guy Debord and Raoul Vaneigem, the great theorists of alienation, alongside theorists of the imagination like Cornelius Castoriadis. For a long time I was genuinely puzzled as to how so many suburban American teenagers could be entranced, for instance, by Raoul Vaneigem's *The Revolution of Everyday Life* – a book, after all, written in Paris almost forty years ago. In the end I decided it must be because Vaneigem's book was, in its own way, the highest theoretical expression of the feelings of rage, boredom, and revulsion that almost any adolescent at some point feels when confronted with the middle class existence. The sense of a life broken into fragments, with no ultimate meaning or integrity; of a cynical market system taking selling its victims commodities and spectacles that themselves represent tiny false images of the very sense of totality and pleasure and community the market has in fact destroyed; the tendency to turn every relation into a form of exchange, to sacrifice life for "survival," pleasure for

6 It is popular nowadays to say that this is new development, as with theories of "immaterial labor." In fact, as noted above, I suspect it has always been the case; Marx's period was unusual in that it was even possible to imagine things otherwise.

renunciation, creativity for hollow homogenous units of power or "dead time" – on some level all this clearly still rings true.

The question though is why. Contemporary social theory offers little explanation. Poststructuralism, which emerged in the immediate aftermath of '68, was largely born of the rejection of this sort of analysis. It is now simple common sense among social theorists that one cannot define a society as "unnatural" unless one assumes that there is some natural way for society to be, "inhuman" unless there is some authentic human essence, that one cannot say that the self is "fragmented" unless it would be possible to have a unified self, and so on. Since these positions are untenable – since there is no natural condition for society, no authentic human essence, no unitary self – theories of alienation have no basis. Taken purely as arguments, these seem difficult to refute.[7] But how then do we account for the experience?

If one really thinks about it, though, the argument is much less powerful than it seems. After all, what are academic theorists saying? They are saying that the idea of a unitary subject, a whole society, a natural order, are unreal. That all these things are simply figments of our imagination. True enough. But then: what else could they be? And why is that a problem?[8] If imagination is indeed a constituent element in the process of how we produce our social and material realities, there is every reason to believe that

---

7 But the result is that "postmodern" alienation theory sees alienation simply as the subjective experience of those who are somehow oppressed, or excluded, whose own self-definition clashes with the definitions imposed by society. For me, this deprives the concept of much of its power: which is to say that the ultimate problem with the system is not that some are excluded from it, but that even the winners do not really win, because the system itself is ultimately incapable of producing a truly unalienated life for anyone.

8 Perhaps from a Critical Realist perspective one could argue that "reality" is precisely that which can be entirely encompassed in our imaginative constructions; however, this is pretty clearly not what they have in mind; anyway, if one is speaking of political ontologies, as I have been, then politics is precisely the domain where it is most difficult to make such distinctions. Anyway, one could well argue that if there is any human essence, it is precisely our capacity to imagine that we have one.

it proceeds through producing images of totality.[9] That's simply how the imagination works. One must be able to imagine one-self and others as integrated subjects in order to be able to pro-duce beings that are in fact endlessly multiple, imagine some sort of coherent, bounded "society" in order to produce that chaotic open-ended network of social relations that actually exists, and so forth. Normally, people seem able to live with the disparity. The question, it seems to me, is why in certain times and places, the recognition of it instead tends to spark rage and despair, feelings that the social world is a hollow travesty or malicious joke. This, I would argue, is the result of that warping and shattering of the imagination that is the inevitable effect of structural violence.

Part IV: On Revolution

THE SITUATIONISTS, LIKE many '60s radicals, wished to strike back through a strategy of direct action: creating "situations" by creative acts of subversion that undermined the logic of the Spectacle and allowed actors to at least momentarily recapture their imagina-tive powers. At the same time, they also felt all this was inevitably leading up to a great insurrectionary moment – "the" revolution, properly speaking. If the events of May '68 showed anything, it was that if one does not aim to seize state power, there can be no such fundamental, one-time break. The main difference between the Situationists and their most avid current readers is that the mil-lenarian element has almost completely fallen away. No one thinks the skies are about to open any time soon. There is a consolation though: that as a result, as close as one can come to experiencing genuine revolutionary freedom, one can begin to experience it im-mediately. Consider the following statement from the CrimethInc collective, probably the most inspiring young anarchist propagan-dists operating in the Situationist tradition today:

> We must make our freedom by cut-
> ting holes in the fabric of this reality, by
> forging new realities which will, in turn,
> fashion us. Putting yourself in new situa-
> tions constantly is the only way to ensure

9 I have already made this case in a book called *Toward an Anthropological Theory of Value*.

> that you make your decisions unencum-
> bered by the inertia of habit, custom, law,
> or prejudice – and it is up to you to create
> these situations
>
> Freedom only exists in the moment of
> revolution. And those moments are not as
> rare as you think. Change, revolutionary
> change, is going on constantly and every-
> where – and everyone plays a part in it,
> consciously or not.

What is this but an elegant statement of the logic of direct action: the defiant insistence on acting as if one is already free? The obvious question is how it can contribute to an overall strategy, one that should lead to a cumulative movement towards a world without states and capitalism. Here, no one is completely sure. Most assume the process could only be one of endless improvisation. Insurrectionary moments there will certainly be. Likely as not, quite a few of them. But they will most likely be one element in a far more complex and multifaceted revolutionary process whose outlines could hardly, at this point, be fully anticipated.

In retrospect, what seems strikingly naïve is the old assumption that a single uprising or successful civil war could, as it were, neutralize the entire apparatus of structural violence, at least within a particular national territory: that within that territory, right-wing realities could be simply swept away, to leave the field open for an untrammeled outpouring of revolutionary creativity. But if so, the truly puzzling thing is that, at certain moments of human history, that appeared to be exactly what was happening. It seems to me that if we are to have any chance of grasping the new, emerging conception of revolution, we need to begin by thinking again about the quality of these insurrectionary moments.

One of the most remarkable things about such moments is how they can seem to burst out of nowhere – and then, often, dissolve away just as quickly. How is it that the same "public" that two months before say, the Paris Commune, or Spanish Civil War, had voted in a fairly moderate social democratic regime will suddenly find itself willing to risk their lives for the same ultra-radicals who received a fraction of the actual vote? Or, to return to May '68, how is it that the same public that seemed to support or at least feel strongly sympathetic toward the student/worker uprising could almost immediately afterwards return to the polls and elect a right-wing government? The most common historical explanations – that the revolutionaries didn't really represent the public or its interests, but that elements of the public perhaps became caught up in some sort of irrational effervescence – seem obviously inadequate. First of all, they assume that 'the public' is an entity with opinions, interests, and allegiances that can be treated as relatively consistent over time. In fact what we call "the public" is created, produced, through specific institutions that allow specific forms of action – taking polls, watching television, voting, signing petitions or writing letters to elected officials or attending public hearings – and not others. These frames of action imply certain ways of talking, thinking, arguing, deliberating. The same "public" that may widely indulge in the use of recreational chemicals may also consistently vote to make such indulgences illegal; the same collection of citizens are likely to come to completely different decisions on questions affecting their communities if organized into a parliamentary system, a system of computerized plebiscites, or a nested series of public assemblies. In fact the entire anarchist project of reinventing direct democracy is premised on assuming this is the case.

To illustrate what I mean, consider that in America, the same collection of people referred to in one context as "the public" can in another be referred to as "the workforce." They become a "workforce," of course, when they are engaged in different sorts of activity. The "public" does not work – at least, a sentence like "most of the American public works in the service industry" would never appear in a magazine or paper – if a journalist were to attempt to write such a sentence, their editor would certain change it.. It is especially odd since the public does apparently have to *go* to work: this is why, as leftist critics often complain, the media will always talk about how, say, a transport strike is likely to inconvenience the public, in their capacity of commuters, but it will never occur to them that those striking are themselves part of the public, or that whether if they succeed in raising wage levels this will be a public benefit. And certainly the "public" does not go out into the streets. Its role is as audience to public spectacles, and consumers of public services. When buying or using goods and services privately supplied, the same collection of individuals become something else ("consumers"), just as in other contexts of action they are re-labeled a "nation," "electorate," or "population."

All these entities are the product of institutions and institutional practices that, in turn, define certain horizons of possibility. Hence when voting in parliamentary elections one might feel obliged to make a "realistic" choice; in an insurrectionary situation, on the other hand, suddenly anything seems possible.

A great deal of recent revolutionary thought essentially asks: what, then, does this collection of people become during such insurrectionary moments? For the last few centuries the conventional answer has been "the people," and all modern legal regimes ultimately trace their legitimacy to moments of "constituent power," when the people rise up, usually in arms, to create a new constitutional order. The insurrectionary paradigm, in fact, is embedded in the very idea of the modern state. A number of European theorists, understanding that the ground has shifted, have proposed a new term, "the multitude," an entity defined not as a mass of individuals but as a network of relations of cooperation; one that cannot by definition become the basis for a new national or bureaucratic state. For me this project is deeply ambivalent.

In the terms I've been developing, what "the public," "the workforce," "consumers," "population" all have in common is that they are brought into being by institutionalized frames of action that are inherently bureaucratic, and therefore, profoundly alienating. Voting booths, television screens, office cubicles, hospitals, the ritual that surrounds them – one might say these are the very machinery of alienation. They are the instruments through which the human imagination is smashed and shattered. Insurrectionary moments are moments when this bureaucratic apparatus is neutralized. Doing so always seems to have the effect of throwing horizons of possibility wide open. This only to be expected if one of the main things that apparatus normally does is to enforce extremely limited ones. (This is probably why, as Rebecca Solnit has so beautifully observed, people often experience something very similar during natural disasters.) This would explain why revolutionary moments always seem to be followed by an outpouring of social, artistic, and intellectual creativity. Normally unequal structures of imaginative identification are disrupted; everyone is experimenting with trying to see the world from unfamiliar points of view. Normally unequal structures of creativity are disrupted; everyone feels not only the right, but usually the immediate practical need to recreate and reimagine everything around them.[10]

Hence the ambivalence of the process of renaming. On the one hand, it is understandable that those who wish to make radical claims would like to know in whose name they are making them. On the other, if what I've been saying is true, the whole project of first invoking a revolutionary "multitude," and then to start looking for the dynamic forces that lie behind it, begins to look a lot like the first step of that very process of institutionalization that must eventually kill the very thing it celebrates. Subjects (publics, peoples, workforces...) are created by specific institutional structures that are essentially frameworks for action. They are what they do. What revolutionaries do is to break existing frames to create new horizons of possibility, an act that then allows a radical restructuring of the social imagination This is perhaps the one form of action that cannot, by definition, be institutionalized. This

---

10 If things are more complicated it's because what happens doesn't happen to individuals, it's a social process. In fact, to a large extent it is a social stripping away of those social constraints that, paradoxically, define us as isolated individuals. After all, for authors ranging from Kierkegaard to Durkheim, the alienation that is the condition of modern life is not the experience of constraints at all but its very opposite. "Alienation" is the anxiety and despair we face when presented with an almost infinite range of choices, in the absence of any larger moral structures through which to make them meaningful. From an activist perspective though this is simply another effect of institutionalized frameworks: most of all, this is what happens when we are used to imagining ourselves primarily as consumers. In the absence of the market, it would be impossible to conceive of "freedom" as a series of choices made in isolation; instead, freedom can only mean the freedom to choose what kind of commitments one wishes to make to others, and, of course, the experience of living under only those constraints one has freely chosen. At any rate, just as during moments of revolution institutionalized structures of statecraft are dissolved into public assemblies and institutionalized structures of labor control melt into self-management, so do consumer markets give way to conviviality and collective celebration. Spontaneous insurrections are almost always experienced by those taking part as carnivals; an experience that those planning mass actions – as we've seen – are often quite self-consciously trying to reproduce.

is why a number of revolutionary thinkers, from Raffaele Laudani in Italy to the *Colectivo Situaciones* in Argentina, have begun to suggest it might be better her to speak not of "constituent" but "destituent power."

IVa: Revolution in Reverse

THERE IS A strange paradox in Marx's approach to revolution. Generally speaking, when Marx speaks of material creativity, he speaks of "production," and here he insists, as I've mentioned, that the defining feature of humanity is that we first imagine things, and then try to bring them into being. When he speaks of social creativity it is almost always in terms of revolution, but here, he insists that imagining something and then trying to bring it into being is precisely what we should never do. That would be utopianism, and for utopianism, he had only withering contempt.

The most generous interpretation, I would suggest, is that Marx on some level understood that the production of people and social relations worked on different principles, but also knew he did not really have a theory of what those principles were. Probably it was only with the rise of feminist theory – that I was drawing on so liberally in my earlier analysis – that it became possible to think systematically about such issues. I might add that it is a profound reflection on the effects of structural violence on the imagination that feminist theory itself was so quickly sequestered away into its own subfield where it has had almost no impact on the work of most male theorists.

It seems to me no coincidence, then, that so much of the real practical work of developing a new revolutionary paradigm in recent years has also been the work of feminism; or anyway, that feminist concerns have been the main driving force in their transformation. In America, the current anarchist obsession with consensus and other forms of directly democratic process traces back directly to organizational issues within the feminist movement. What had begun, in the late '60s and early '70s, as small, intimate, often anarchist-inspired collectives were thrown into crisis when they started growing rapidly in size. Rather than abandon the search for consensus in decision-making, many began trying to develop more formal versions on the same principles. This, in turn, inspired some radical Quakers (who had previously seen their own consensus decision-making as primarily a religious practice) to begin creating training collectives. By the time of the direct action campaigns against the nuclear power industry in the late '70s, the whole apparatus of affinity groups, spokescouncils, consensus and facilitation had already begun to take something like it's contemporary form. The resulting outpouring of new forms of consensus process constitutes the most important contribution to revolutionary practice in decades. It is largely the work of feminists engaged in practical organizing – a majority, probably, feminists tied at least loosely the anarchist tradition, or at least more and more as mainstream feminism turned away from the politics of direct action and anarchism came to take on such processes as its own. This makes it all the more ironic that male theorists who have not themselves engaged in on-the-ground organizing or taken part in anarchist decision-making processes, but who find themselves drawn to anarchism as a principle, so often feel obliged to include in otherwise sympathetic statements, that of course they don't agree with this obviously impractical, pie-in-the-sky, unrealistic consensus nonsense.

The organization of mass actions themselves – festivals of resistance, as they are often called – can be considered pragmatic experiments in whether it is indeed possible to institutionalize the experience of liberation, the giddy realignment of imaginative powers, everything that is most powerful in the experience of a successful spontaneous insurrection. Or if not to institutionalize it, perhaps, to produce it on call. The effect for those involved is as if everything were happening in reverse. A revolutionary uprising begins with battles in the streets, and if successful, proceeds to outpourings of popular effervescence and festivity. There follows the sober business of creating new institutions, councils, decision-making processes, and ultimately the reinvention of everyday life. Such at least is the ideal, and certainly there have been moments in human history where something like that has begun to happen – much though, again, such spontaneous creations always seems to end being subsumed within some new form of violent bureaucracy. However, as I've noted, this is more or less inevitable since bureaucracy, however much it serves as the immediate organizer of situations of power and structural blindness, does not create them. Mainly, it simply evolves to manage them.

This is one reason direct action proceeds in the opposite direction. Probably a majority of the participants are drawn from subcultures that are all about reinventing everyday life. Even if not, actions begin with the creation of new forms of collective decision-making: councils, assemblies, the endless attention to 'process' – and uses those forms to plan the street actions and popular festivities. The result is, usually, a dramatic confrontation with armed representatives of the state. While most organizers would be delighted to see things escalate to a popular insurrection, and something like that does occasionally happen, most would not expect these to mark any kind of permanent breaks in reality. They serve more as something almost along the lines of momentary advertisements – or better, foretastes, experiences of visionary inspiration – for a much slower, painstaking struggle of creating alternative institutions.

One of the most important contributions of feminism, it seems to me, has been to constantly remind everyone that "situations" do not create themselves. There is usually a great deal of work involved. For much of human history, what has been taken as politics has consisted essentially of a series of dramatic performances carried out upon theatrical stages. One of the great gifts of feminism to political thought has been to continually remind us of the people is in fact making and preparing and cleaning those stages, and even more, maintaining the invisible structures that make them possible – people who have, overwhelmingly, been women. The normal process of politics of course is to make such people disappear. Indeed one of the chief functions of women's work is to make *itself* disappear. One might say that the political ideal within direct action circles has become to efface the difference; or, to put it another way, that action is seen as genuinely revolutionary when the process of production of situations is experienced as just as liberating as the situations themselves. It is an experiment one might say in the realignment of imagination, of creating truly non-alienated forms of experience.

Conclusion

OBVIOUSLY IT IS also attempting to do so in a context in which, far from being put in temporary abeyance, state power (in many parts of the globe at least) so suffuses every aspect of daily existence that its armed representatives intervene to regulate the internal organizational structure of groups allowed to cash checks or own and operate motor vehicles. One of the remarkable things about the current, neoliberal age is that bureaucracy has come to so all-encompassing – this period has seen, after all, the creation of the first effective global administrative system in human history – that we don't even see it any more. At the same time, the pressures of operating within a context of endless regulation, repression, sexism, racial and class dominance, tend to ensure many who get drawn into the politics of direct action experience a constant alteration of exaltation and burn-out, moments where everything seems possible alternating with moments where nothing does. In other parts of the world, autonomy is much easier to achieve, but at the cost of isolation or almost complete absence of resources. How to create alliances between different zones of possibility is a fundamental problem.

These however are questions of strategy that go well beyond the scope of the current essay. My purpose here has been more modest. Revolutionary theory, it seems to me, has in many fronts advanced much less quickly than revolutionary practice; my aim in writing this has been to see if one could work back from the experience of direct action to begin to create some new theoretical tools. They are hardly meant to be definitive. They may not even prove useful. But perhaps they can contribute to a broader project of re-imagining.

Army of Altruists

> *You know, education, if you make the most*
> *of it, you study hard, you do your homework*
> *and you make an effort to be smart, you can*
> *do well. If you don't, you get stuck in Iraq.*
>
> John Kerry (D-Mass.)

> *Kerry owes an apology to the many thousands of*
> *Americans serving in Iraq, who answered their*
> *country's call because they are patriots and not*
> *because of any deficiencies in their education.*
>
> John McCain (R-Ariz.)

THE ONE FLEETING MOMENT OF HOPE FOR REPUBLICANS DUR-
ing the lead-up to the 2006 congressional elections came was afforded by a lame joke by Senator John Kerry – a joke pretty obviously aimed at George Bush – which they took to suggest that
Kerry thought that only those who flunked out of school end up in
the military. It was all very disingenuous. Most knew perfectly well
Kerry's real point was to suggest the President wasn't very bright.
But the right smelled blood. The problem with "aristo-slackers"

like Kerry, wrote one National Review blogger, is that they assume "the troops are in Iraq not because they are deeply committed to the mission (they need to deny that) but rather because of a system that takes advantage of their lack of social and economic opportunities... We should clobber them with that ruthlessly until the day of the election – just like we did in '04 – because it is the most basic reason they deserve to lose."

As it turned out, it didn't make a lot of difference, because most Americans decided they were not deeply committed to the mission either – insofar as they were even sure what the mission was. But it seems to me the question we should really be asking is: why did it take a military catastrophe (and a strategy of trying to avoid any association with the kind of northeastern elites Kerry for so many typified) to allow the congressional democrats to finally come out of the political wilderness? Or even more: why has this Republican line proved so effective?

It strikes me that to get at the answer, one has to probe far more deeply into the nature of American society than most commentators, nowadays, are willing to go. We're used to reducing all such issues to an either/or: patriotism versus opportunity, values versus bread-and-butter issues like jobs and education. It seems to me though that just framing things this way plays into the hands of the Right. Certainly, most people do join the army because they are deprived of opportunities. But the real question to be asking is: opportunities to do what?

I'm an anthropologist and what follows might be considered an anthropological perspective on the question. It first came home to me a year or two ago when I was attending a lecture by Catherine Lutz, a fellow anthropologist from Brown who has been studying U.S. military bases overseas. Many of these bases organize outreach programs, in which soldiers venture out to repair schoolrooms or to perform free dental checkups for the locals. These programs were created to improve local relations, but in this task they often proved remarkably ineffective. Why, then, did the army not abandon them? The answer was that the programs had such enormous psychological impact on the soldiers, many of whom would wax euphoric when describing them: e.g., "*This* is why I joined the army"; "This is what military service is really all about – not just defending your country, but helping people." Professor Lutz is convinced that the main reason these programs continue to be funded is that soldiers who take part in them are more likely to reenlist. The military's own statistics are no help here: the surveys do not list "helping people" among the motive for reenlistment. Interestingly, it is the most high-minded option available – "patriotism" – that is the overwhelming favorite.

Certainly, Americans do not see themselves as a nation of frustrated altruists. Quite the opposite: our normal habits of thought tend towards a rough and ready cynicism. The world is a giant marketplace; everyone is in it for a buck; if you want to understand why something happened, first ask who stands to gain by it. The same attitudes expressed in the back rooms of bars are echoed in the highest reaches of social science. America's great contribution to the world in the latter respect has been the development of "rational choice" theories, which proceed from the assumption that all human behavior can be understood as a matter of economic calculation, of rational actors trying to get as much as possible out of any given situation with the least cost to themselves. As a result, in most fields, the very existence of altruistic behavior is considered a kind of puzzle, and everyone from economists to evolutionary biologists have made themselves famous through attempts to "solve" it – that is, to explain the mystery of why bees sacrifice themselves for hives or human beings hold open doors and give correct street directions to total strangers. At the same time, the case of the military bases suggests the possibility that in fact Americans, particularly the less affluent ones, are haunted by frustrated desires to do good in the world.

It would not be difficult to assemble evidence that this is the case. Studies of charitable giving, for example, have always shown the poor to be the most generous: the lower one's income, the higher the proportion of it that one is likely to give away to strangers. The same pattern holds true, incidentally, when comparing the middle classes and the rich: one study of tax returns in 2003 concluded that if the most affluent families had given away as much of their assets even as the average middle class family, overall charitable donations that year would have increased by 25 billion dollars. (All this despite the fact the wealthy have far more time and opportunity.) Moreover, charity represents only a tiny part of the picture. If one were to break down what the typical American wage earner does with his money one would likely find they give most of it away. Take a typical male head of household. About a third of his annual income is likely to end up being redistributed to strangers, through taxes and charity – another third he is likely to give in one way or another to his children; of the remainder, probably the largest part is given to or shared with others: presents, trips, parties, the six-pack of beer for the local softball game. One might object that this latter is more a reflection of the real nature of pleasure than anything else (who would want to eat a delicious meal at an expensive restaurant all by themselves?) but itself this is half the point. Even our self-indulgences tend to be dominated by the logic of the gift. Similarly, some might object that shelling out a small fortune to send one's children to an exclusive kindergarten is more about status than altruism. Perhaps: but if you look at what happens over the course of people's actual lives, it soon becomes apparent this kind of behavior fulfills an identical psychological need. How many youthful idealists throughout history have managed to finally come to terms with a world based on selfishness and greed the moment they start a family? If one were to assume altruism were the primary human motivation, this would make perfect sense: The only way they can convince themselves to abandon their desire to do right by the world as a whole is to substitute an even more powerful desire do right by their children.

What all this suggests to me is that American society might well work completely differently than we tend to assume. Imagine, for a moment, that the United States as it exists today were the creation of some ingenious social engineer. What assumptions about human nature could we say this engineer must have been working with? Certainly nothing like rational choice theory. For clearly our social engineer understands that the only way to convince human beings to enter into the world of work and the marketplace (that is: of mind-numbing labor and cut-throat competition) is to dangle the prospect of thereby being able to lavish money on one's children, buy drinks for one's friends, and, if one hits the jackpot, to be able to spend the rest of one's life endowing museums and providing AIDS medications to impoverished countries in Africa. Where our theorists are constantly trying to strip away the veil of appearances and show how all such apparently selfless gesture really mask some kind of self-interested strategy, in reality, American society is better conceived as a battle over access to the right to behave altruistically. Selflessness – or at least, the right to engage in high-minded activity – is not the strategy. It is the prize.

If nothing else, I think this helps us understand why the Right has been so much better, in recent years, at playing to populist sentiments than the Left. Essentially, they do it by accusing liberals of cutting ordinary Americans off from the right to do good in the world. Let me explain what I mean here by throwing out a series of propositions.

PROPOSITION I:
Neither egoism nor altruism are natural urges; they are in fact arise in relation to one another and neither would be conceivable without the market.

FIRST OF ALL, I should make clear that I do not believe that either egoism or altruism are somehow inherent to human nature. Human motives are rarely that simple. Rather egoism or altruism are ideas we have about human nature. Historically, one tends to arise in response to the other. In the ancient world, for example, it is precisely in the times and places as one sees the emergence of money and markets that one also sees the rise of world religions – Buddhism, Christianity, and Islam. If one sets aside a space and says, "Here you shall think only about acquiring material things for yourself," then it is hardly surprising that before long someone else will set aside a countervailing space, declaring, in effect: "Yes, but *here*, we must contemplate the fact that the self, and material things, are ultimately unimportant." It was these latter institutions, of course, that first developed our modern notions of charity.

Even today, when we operate outside the domain of the market or of religion, very few of our actions could be said to be motivated by anything so simple as untrammeled greed or utterly selfless generosity. When we are dealing not with strangers but with friends, relatives, or enemies, a much more complicated set of motivations will generally come into play: envy, solidarity, pride, self-destructive grief, loyalty, romantic obsession, resentment, spite, shame, conviviality, the anticipation of shared enjoyment, the desire to show up a rival, and so on. These are the motivations that impel the major dramas of our lives, that great novelists like Tolstoy and Dostoevsky immortalize, but that social theorists, for some reason, tend to ignore. If one travels to parts of the world where money and markets do not exist – say, to certain parts of

New Guinea or Amazonia – such complicated webs of motivation are precisely what one still finds. In societies where most people live in small communities, where almost everyone they know is either a friend, a relative or an enemy, the languages spoken tend even to lack words that correspond to "self-interest" or "altruism," while including very subtle vocabularies for describing envy, solidarity, pride and the like. Their economic dealings with one another likewise tend to be based on much more subtle principles. Anthropologists have created a vast literature to try to fathom the dynamics of these apparently exotic "gift economies," but if it seems odd to us to see, say, important men conniving with their cousins to finagle vast wealth, which they then present as gifts to bitter enemies in order to publicly humiliate them, it is because we are so used to operating inside impersonal markets that it never occurs to us to think how we would act if we had an economic system where we treated people based on how we actually felt about them.

Nowadays, the work of destroying such ways of life is largely left to missionaries – representatives of those very world religions that originally sprung up in reaction to the market long ago. Missionaries, of course, are out to save souls; but this rarely interpret this to mean their role is simply to teach people to accept God and be more altruistic. Almost invariably, they end up trying to convince people to be more selfish, and more altruistic, at the same time. On the one hand, they set out to teach the "natives" proper work discipline, and try to get them involved with buying and selling products on the market, so as to better their material lot. At the same time, they explain to them that ultimately, material things are unimportant, and lecture on the value of the higher things, such as selfless devotion to others.

PROPOSITION II:
The political right has always tried to enhance this division, and thus claim to be champions of egoism and altruism simultaneously. The left has tried to efface it.
MIGHT THIS NOT help to explain why the United States, the most market-driven industrialized society on earth, is also the most religious? Or, even more strikingly, why the country that produced Tolstoy and Dostoevsky spent much of the twentieth century trying to eradicate both the market and religion entirely?

Where the political left has always tried to efface this distinction – whether by trying to create economic systems that are not driven by the profit motive, or by replacing private charity with one or another form community support – the political right has always thrived on it. In the United States, for example, the Republican party is dominated by two ideological wings: the libertarians, and the "Christian right." At one extreme, Republicans are free-market fundamentalists and advocates of individual liberties (even if they see those liberties largely as a matter of consumer choice); on the other, they are fundamentalists of a more literal variety, suspicious of most individual liberties but enthusiastic about biblical injunctions, "family values," and charitable good works. At first glance it might seem remarkable such an alliance manages to hold together at all (and certainly they have ongoing tensions, most famously over abortion). But in fact right-wing coalitions almost always take some variation of this form. One might say that the conservative approach always has been to release the dogs of the market, throwing all traditional verities into disarray; and then, in this tumult of insecurity, offering themselves up as the last bastion of order and hierarchy, the stalwart defenders of the authority of churches and fathers against the barbarians they have themselves unleashed. A scam it may be, but a remarkably effective one; and one effect is that the right ends up seeming to have a monopoly on value. They manage, we might say, to occupy both positions, on either side of the divide: extreme egoism and extreme altruism.

Consider, for a moment, the word "value." When economists talk about value they are really talking about money – or more precisely, about whatever it is that money is measuring; also, whatever it is that economic actors are assumed to be pursuing. When we are working for a living, or buying and selling things, we are rewarded with money. But whenever we are not working or buying or selling, when we are motivated by pretty much anything other the desire to get money, we suddenly find ourselves in the domain of "values." The most commonly invoked of these are of course "family values" (which is unsurprising, since by far the most common form of unpaid labor in most industrial societies is child-rearing and housework), but we also talk about religious values, political values, the values that attach themselves to art or patriotism – one could even, perhaps, count loyalty to one's favorite basketball team. All are seen as commitments that are, or ought to be, uncorrupted by the market. At the same time, they are also seen as utterly unique; where money makes all things comparable, "values" such as beauty, devotion, or integrity cannot, by definition, be compared. There is no mathematic formula that could possibly allow one to calculate just how much personal integrity it is right to sacrifice in the pursuit of art, or how to balance responsibilities to your family with responsibilities to your God. (Obviously, people do make these kind of compromises all the time. But they cannot be calculated). One might put it this way: if value is simply what one considers important, then money allows importance take a liquid form, enables us to compare precise quantities of importance and trade one off for the other. After all, if someone does accumulate a very large amount of money, the first thing they are likely to do is to try to convert it into something unique, whether this be Monet's water lilies, a prize-winning racehorse, or an endowed chair at a university.

What is really at stake here in any market economy is precisely the ability to make these trades, to convert "value" into "values." We all are striving to put ourselves in a position where we can dedicate ourselves to something larger than ourselves. When liberals do well in America, it's because they can embody that possibility: the Kennedys, for example, are the ultimate Democratic icons not just because they started as poor Irish immigrants who made enormous amounts of money, but because they are seen as having managed, ultimately, to turn all that money into nobility.

PROPOSITION III:
The real problem of the American left is that while it does try in certain ways to efface the division between egoism and altruism, value and values, it largely does so for its own children. This has allowed the right to paradoxically represent itself as the champions of the working class.

ALL THIS MIGHT help explain why the Left in America is in such a mess. Far from promoting new visions of effacing the difference between egoism and altruism, value and values, or providing a model for passing from one to the other, progressives cannot even seem to think their way past it. After the last presidential election, the big debate in progressive circles was the relative importance of economic issues versus what was called "the culture wars." Did the Democrats lose because they were not able to spell out any plausible economic alternatives, or did the Republicans win because they successfully mobilized conservative Christians around the issue of gay marriage? As I say, the very fact that progressives frame the question this way not only shows they are trapped in the right's terms of analysis. It demonstrates they do not understand how America really works.

Let me illustrate what I mean by considering the strange popular appeal, at least until recently, of George W. Bush. In 2004, most of the American liberal intelligentsia did not seem to be able to get their heads around it. After the election, what left so many of them reeling was their suspicion that the things they most hated about Bush were exactly what so many Bush voters liked about him. Consider the debates, for example. If statistics are to be believed, millions of Americans who watched George Bush and John Kerry lock horns, concluded that Kerry won, and then went off and voted for Bush anyway. It was hard to escape the suspicion that in the end, Kerry's articulate presentation, his skill with words and arguments, had actually counted against him.

This sends liberals into spirals of despair. They cannot understand why decisive leadership is equated with acting like an idiot. Neither can they understand how a man who comes from one of the most elite families in the country, who attended Andover, Yale, and Harvard, and whose signature facial expression is a self-satisfied smirk, could ever convince anyone he was a "man of the people." I must admit I have struggled with this as well. As a child of working class parents who won a scholarship to Andover in the 1970s and eventually, a job at Yale, I have spent much of my life in the presence of men like Bush., everything about them oozing self-satisfied privilege. But in fact, stories like mine – stories of dramatic class mobility through academic accomplishment – are increasingly unusual in America.

America of course continues to see itself as a land of opportunity, and certainly from the perspective of an immigrant from Haiti or Bangladesh, it is. No doubt in terms of overall social mobility, we still compare favorably to countries like Bolivia or France. But America has always been a country built on the promise of *unlimited* upward mobility. The working-class condition has been traditionally seen as a way station, as something one's family passes through on the road to something better. Lincoln used to stress that what made American democracy possible was the absence of a class of permanent wage laborers. In Lincoln's day, the ideal was that it was mainly immigrants who worked as wage laborers, and that they did so in order to save up enough money to do something else: if nothing else, to buy some land and become a homesteader on the frontier.

The point is not how accurate this ideal was; the point was most Americans have found the image plausible. Every time the road is perceived to be clogged, profound unrest ensues. The closing of the frontier led to bitter labor struggles, and over the course of the twentieth century, the steady and rapid expansion of the American university system could be seen as a kind of substitute. Particularly after World War II, huge resources were poured into expanding the higher education system, which grew extremely rapidly, and all this was promoted quite explicitly as a means of social mobility. This served during the Cold War as almost an implied social contract, not just offering a comfortable life to the working classes but holding out the chance that their children would not be working-class themselves.

The problem, of course, is that a higher education system cannot be expanded forever. At a certain point one ends up with a significant portion of the population unable to find work even remotely in line with their qualifications, who have every reason to be angry about their situation, and who also have access to the entire history of radical thought. During the twentieth century, this was precisely the situation most likely to spark revolts and insurrections – revolutionary heroes from Chairman Mao to Fidel Castro almost invariably turn out to be children of poor parents who scrimped to give their children a bourgeois education, only to discover that a bourgeois education does not, in itself, guarantee entry into the bourgeoisie. By the late sixties and early seventies, the very point where the expansion of the university system hit a dead end, campuses were, predictably, exploding.

What followed could be seen as a kind of settlement. Campus radicals were reabsorbed into the university, but set to work largely at training children of the elite. As the cost of education has skyrocketed, financial aid has been cut back, and the government has begun aggressively pursuing student loan debts that once existed largely on paper, the prospect of social mobility through education – above all liberal arts education – has been rapidly diminished. The number of working-class students in major universities, which steadily grew until at least the late sixties, has now been declining for decades.

If working-class Bush voters tend to resent intellectuals more than they do the rich, then, the most likely reason is because they can imagine scenarios in which they might become rich, but cannot imagine one in which they, or any of their children, could ever become members of the intelligentsia? If you think about it, this is not an unreasonable assessment. A mechanic from Nebraska knows it is highly unlikely that his son or daughter will ever become an Enron executive. But it is possible. There is virtually no chance on the other hand that his child, no matter how talented, will ever become an international human rights lawyer, or a drama critic for the *New York Times*. Here we need to remember not just the changes in higher education, but also the role that unpaid, or effectively unpaid, internships. It has become a fact of life in the United States that if one chooses a career for any reason other than the money, for the first year or two one will not be paid. This is certainly true if one wishes to be involved in altruistic pursuits: say, to join the world of charities, or NGOs, or to become a political activist. But it is equally true if one wants to pursue values like Beauty or Truth: to become part of the world of books, or the art world, or an investigative reporter. The custom effectively seals off any such career for any poor student who actually does attain a liberal arts education. Such structures of exclusion had always existed of course, especially at the top, but in recent decades fences have become fortresses.

If that mechanic's son – or daughter – wishes to pursue something higher, more noble, for a career, what options does she really have? Likely just two. She can seek employment with her local church, which is hard to get. Or she can join the Army.

This is, of course, the secret of nobility. To be noble is to be generous, high-minded, altruistic, to pursue higher forms of value. But it is also to be able to do so because one does not really have to think too much about money. This is precisely what our soldiers are doing when they give free dental examinations to villagers: they are being paid (modestly, but adequately) to do good in the world. Seen in this light, it is also easier to see what really happened at universities in the wake of the 1960s – the "settlement" I mentioned above. Campus radicals set out to create a new society that destroyed the distinction between egoism and altruism, value and values. It did not work out, but they were, effectively, offered a kind of compensation: the privilege to use the university system to create lives that did so, in their own little way, to be supported in one's material needs while pursuing virtue, truth, and beauty, and above all, to pass that privilege on to their own children. One cannot blame them for accepting the offer. But neither can one blame the rest of the country for resenting the hell out of them. Not because they reject the project: as I say, this is what America is all about.

As I always tell activists engaged in the peace movement and counter-recruitment campaigns: why do working class kids join the Army anyway? Because like any teenager, they want to escape the world of tedious work and meaningless consumerism, to live a life of adventure and camaraderie in which they believe they are doing something genuinely noble. They join the Army because they want to be like you.

The Sadness of Post-workerism

ON JANUARY 19TH, 2007 SEVERAL OF THE HEAVYWEIGHTS OF
Italian post-Workerist theory – Toni Negri, Franco 'Bifo' Berardi,
Maurizio Lazzarato, and Judith Revel – appeared at the Tate
Modern to talk about art. This is a review.

Or, it is a review in a certain sense. I want to give an account
of what happened. But I also want to talk about why I think
what happened was interesting and important. For me at least,
this means addressing not only what was said but just as much,
perhaps, what wasn't; and asking questions like "why immaterial labor ?," and "why did it make sense to the organizers
– indeed, to all concerned – to bring a group of revolutionary
theorists over from Italy to London to talk about art history in
the first place?" Asking these questions will allow me to make
some much broader points about the nature of art, politics, history, and social theory, which I like to think are at least as interesting and potentially revealing than what happened in the
actual debate.

What happened

Here's a very brief summary:

The session was organized by Peter Osborne, along with a number of other scholars at Middlesex College involved in the journal *Radical Philosophy*, and Eric Alliez, editor of *Multitudes*. None of the organizers could really be considered part of the art world. Neither were any of the speakers known primarily for what they had to say about things artistic. Everyone seems to have felt they were there to explore slightly new territory. This included, I think, much of the audience. The place was packed, but especially, it seemed, with students and scholars involved in some way with post-graduate education – especially where it interfaced with the culture industry. Among many scholars, especially younger ones, some of the speakers – especially Negri – were very big names, celebrities, even something close to rock stars. Many of the graduate students were no doubt there in part just for the opportunity to finally see figures whose ideas they'd been debating for most of their intellectual careers revealed in to them in the flesh: to see what they looked like, what kind of clothes they wore, how they held themselves and spoke and moved. Perhaps even to mill about in the pub afterwards and rub shoulders.

This is always part of the pleasure of the event. Certainly this was part of the pleasure for me. Great theorists are almost always, in a certain sense, performers. Even if you've seen photographs, it never conveys a full sense of who they are; and when you do get a sense of who they are, returning to read their work with one's new, personal sense of the author tends to be an entirely different experience. It was interesting to observe Lazzarato's smooth head and excellent moustache; Revel's poise and energy; Bifo's hair – sort of Warhol meets Jacques Derrida – not to mention the way he seemed to walk as if floating a half inch above the pavement; Negri's almost sheepishness at his inability to pronounce long English words, which made him seem shy and almost boyish. I had never really had a sense of what any of these people were like and I walked away, oddly, with much more respect for them as people. This is partly no doubt because anyone who you know largely through obscurely written texts that some treat with an almost mystical adulation tends to become, in one's imagination, rather an arrogant person, self-important, someone who thinks oneself a kind of minor rock star, perhaps, since they are treated as such – even if within a very narrow circle. Events like this remind one just how narrow the circle of such celebrity can often be. These were people who certainly were comfortable in the spotlight. But otherwise, their conditions of existence obviously in no way resembled that of rock stars. In fact they were rather modest. Most had paid a significant price for their radical commitments and some continued to do so: Negri is now out of jail of course and settled in a fairly comfortable life on academic and government pensions, but Bifo is a high school teacher (if at a very classy high school) and Lazzarato appears under the dreaded rubric of "independent scholar." It's a little shocking to discover scholars of such recognized importance in the domain of ideas could really have received such little institutional recognition, but of course (as I would know better than anyone), there is very little connection between the two – especially, when politics is involved.

(Neither were they likely to be walking home with vast troves of money from taking part in this particular event: 500 tickets at £20 each might seem like a bit of money, but once you figure in the cost of the venue, hotels and transportation, the remainder, split four ways, would make for a decidedly modest lecture fee.)

All in all, they seemed to exude an almost wistful feeling, of modest, likable people scratching their heads over the knowledge that, twenty years before, struggling side to side with insurrectionary squatters and running pirate radio stations, they would never have imagined ending up quite where they were now, filling the lecture hall of a stodgy British museum with philosophy students eager to hear their opinions about art. The wistfulness was only intensified by the general tenor of the afternoon's discussion, which started off guardedly hopeful about social possibilities in the first half, and then, in the second half, collapsed.

Here's a brief summary of what happened:

• MAURIZIO LAZZARATO presented a paper called **'Art, Work and Politics in Disciplinary Societies and Societies of Security',** in which he talked about Duchamp and Kafka's story Josephine the singing mouse, and explained how the relation of "art, work, and politics" had changed as we pass from Foucault's "disciplinary society" to his "society of security." Duchamp's ready-mades provides a kind of model of a new form of action that lies suspended between what we consider production and management; it is an anti-dialectical model in effect of forms of immaterial labor to follow, which entail just the sort of blurring of boundaries of work and play, art and life that the avant garde had called for, that is opened up in the spaces of freedom that "societies of security" must necessarily allow, and that any revolutionary challenge to capitalism must embrace.

• **JUDITH REVEL** presented a paper called '**The Material of the Immaterial: Against the Return of Idealisms and New Vitalisms**', explained that even many of those willing to agree that we are now under a regime of real subsumption to capital do not seem to fully understand the implications: that there is *nothing* outside. This includes those who posit some sort of autonomous life-force, such as Agamben's "bare life." Such ideas need to be jettisoned, as also Deleuze's insistence we see desire as a vital energy prior to the constraints of power. Rather, the current moment can be understood only through Foucault, particularly his notion of ethical self-fashioning; this also allows us to see that art is not a series of objects but a form of critical practice designed to produce ruptures in existing regimes of power.

> • **a lively discussion** ensued in which everyone seemed happy to declare Agamben defunct but the Deleuzians fought back bitterly. No clear victor emerged

• **BIFO** presented a paper called '**Connection/Conjunction.**' He began by talking about Marinetti and Futurism. The twentieth century was the "century of the future." But that's over. In the current moment, which is no longer one of conjunction but of connection, there is no longer a future. Cyber-space is infinite, but cyber-time is most definitively not. The precarity of labor means life is pathologized; and where once Lenin could teeter back and forth from depressive breakdowns to decisive historical action, no such action is now possible, suicide is the only form of effective political action; art and life have fused and it's a disaster; any new wave of radical subjectification is inconceivable now. If there was hope, it is only for some great catastrophe, after which possibly, maybe, everything might change.

> ◆ **a confused and depressing discussion** ensued, in which Bifo defended his despair, in a cheerful and charming manner, admitting that he has abandoned Deleuze for Baudrillard. There's no hope, he says. "I hope that I am wrong."

◆ **TONI NEGRI** presented a paper called **'Concerning Periodisation in Art: Some Approaches to Art and Immaterial Labour'** which began, as the title implies, with a brief history of how, since the 1840s, artistic trends mirrored changes in the composition of labor. (That part was really quite lucid. Then the words began.) Then after '68, we had Post-Modernism, but now we're beyond that too, all the posts are post now, we're in yet a new phase: Contemporaneity, in which we see the ultimate end of cognitive labor is prosthesis, the simultaneous genesis of person and machine; as biopolitical power it becomes a constant explosion, a vital excess beyond measure, through which the multitude's powers can take ethical form in the creation of a new global commons. Despite the occasional explosive metaphors, the talk was received as a gesture of quiet but determined revolutionary optimism opposing itself to Bifo's grandiose gesture of despair – if one diluted, somewhat, by the fact that almost no one in the audience seemed able to completely understand it. While the first, analytical part of the paper was admirably concrete, as soon as the argument moved to revolutionary prospects, it also shifted to a level of abstraction so arcane that it was almost impossible for this listener, at least (and I took copious notes!) to figure out what, exactly, any of this would mean in practice.

> ◆ **a final discussion was proposed** in which each speaker was asked to sum up. There is a certain

reluctance. Lazzarato demurs, he does not want to say anything. "Bifo has made me depressed." Bifo too passes. Negri admits that Bifo has indeed defined the "heaviest, most burdensome" question of our day, but all, he insists, is not necessarily lost, rather, a new language is required to even begin to think about such matters. Only Judith Revel picks up the slack noting, despite all the miserable realities of the world, the power of our indignation is also real – the only question is, how to transform that power into the Common

Revel's intervention, however, had something of the air of a desperate attempt to save the day. Everyone left confused, and a bit unsettled. Bifo's collapse of faith was particularly unsettling because generally he is the very avatar of hope; in fact, even here his manner and argument seemed at almost complete cross-purposes with one another, his every gesture exuding a kind of playful energy, a delight in the fact of existence, that his every word seemed determined to puncture and negate. It was very difficult to know what to make of it.

Instead of trying to take on the arguments point by point – as I said, this is only a sort of review – let me instead throw out some initial thoughts on what the presentations had in common. In other words, I am less interested in entering into the ring and batting around arguments for whether Foucault or Deleuze are better suited for helping us realize the radical potential in the current historical moment, as to why such questions are being batted about by Italian revolutionaries, in an art museum, in the first place. Here I can make four initial observations, all of which, at the time, I found mildly surprising:

1) There was almost no discussion of contemporary art. Just about every piece of art discussed was within what might be called the classic avant garde tradition (Dada, Futurism, Duchamp, Abstract Expressionism...) Negri did take his history of art forms up through the '60s, and Bifo mentioned Banksy. But that was about it.

2) While all of the speakers could be considered Italian autonomists and they were ostensibly there to discuss Immaterial Labor, a concept that emerged from the Italian autonomist (aka Post-Workerist) tradition, surprisingly few concepts specific to that tradition were deployed. Rather, the theoretical language drew almost exclusively on the familiar heroes of French '68 thought: Michel Foucault, Jean Baudrillard, Deleuze and Guattari... At one point, the editor of *Multitudes*, Eric Alliez, in introducing Negri made a point of saying that one of the great achievements of his work was to give a second life to such thinkers, a kind of renewed street cred, by making them seem once again relevant to revolutionary struggle.

3) In each case, the presenters used those French thinkers as a tool to create a theory about historical stages – or some cases, imitated them by coming up with an analogous theory of stages of their own. For each, the key question was: What is the right term with which characterize the present? What makes our time unique? Is it that we have passed from a society of discipline, to one of security, or control? Or is it that regimes of conjunction been replaced by regimes of connection? Have we experienced a passage from formal to real subsumption? Or from modernity to postmodernity? Or have we passed postmodernity too, now, and entered an entirely new phase?

4) Everyone was remarkably polite. Dramatically lacking were bold, rebellious statements, or really anything likely to provoke discomfort in even the stodgiest Tate Britain curator, or for that matter any of their wealthy Tory patrons. This is worthy of note since no one can seriously deny the speakers' radical credentials. Most had proved themselves willing to take genuine personal risks at moments when there was reason to believe some realistic prospect of revolution was afoot. True, that was some time ago (Negri got himself in trouble mainly in the '70s), but still: there was no doubt that, had some portion of London's proletariat risen up in arms during their stay, most if not all would have reported to the barricades. But

since they had not, their attacks or even criticisms were
limited to other intellectuals: Badiou, Ranciere, Agamben.

These observations may seem scattershot but taken together, I
think they are revealing. Why, for example, would one wish to argue that in the year 2008 we live in a unique historical moment,
unlike anything that came before, and then act as if this moment
can only really be described through concepts French thinkers developed in the 1960s and '70s – then go on to illustrate one's points
almost exclusively with art created between 1916 and 1922?

This does seem strangely arbitrary. Still, I suspect there is a
reason. We might ask: what does the moment of Futurism, Dada,
Constructivism and the rest, and French '68 thought, have in common? Actually quite a lot. Each corresponded to a moment of revolution: to adopt Immanuel Wallerstein's terminology, the world
revolution of 1917 in one case, and the world revolution of 1968
in the other. Each witnessed an explosion of creativity in which
a longstanding European artistic or intellectual Grand Tradition
effectively reached the limits of its radical possibilities. That is to
say, they marked the last moment at which it was possible to plau-
sibly claim that breaking all the rules – whether violating artistic
conventions, or shattering philosophical assumptions – was itself,
necessarily, a subversive political act as well.

This is particularly easy to see in the case of the European avant
garde. From Duchamp's first readymade in 1914, Hugo Ball's Dada
manifesto and tone poems in 1916, to Malevich's White on White
in 1918, culminating in the whole phenomenon of Berlin Dada
from 1918 to 1922, one could see revolutionary artists perform,
in rapid succession, just about every subversive gesture it was
possible to make: from white canvases to automatic writing, theatrical performances designed to incite riots, sacrilegious photo
montage, gallery shows in which the public was handed hammers
and invited to destroy any piece they took a disfancy to, to objects plucked off the street and sacralized as art. All that remained
for the Surrealists was to connect a few remaining dots, and after
that, the heroic moment was definitely over. One could still do
political art, of course, and one could still defy convention. But it
became effectively impossible to claim that by doing one you were
necessarily doing the other, and increasingly difficult to even try
to do both at the same time. It was possible, certainly, to continue

in the Avant Garde tradition without claiming one's work had political implications (as did anyone from Jackson Pollock to Andy Warhol), it was possible to do straight-out political art (like, say, Diego Rivera); one could even (like the Situationists) continue as a revolutionary in the Avant Garde tradition but stop making art, but that pretty much exhausted the remaining possibilities.

What happened to Continental philosophy after May '68 is quite similar. Assumptions were shattered, grand declarations abounded (the intellectual equivalent of Dada manifestos): the death of Man, of Truth, The Social, Reason, Dialectics, even Death itself. But the end result was roughly the same. Within a decade, the possible radical positions one could take within the Grand Tradition of post-Cartesian philosophy had been, essentially, exhausted. The heroic moment was over. What's more, it became increasingly difficult to maintain the premise that heroic acts of epistemological subversion were revolutionary or even, particularly subversive in any other sense. Their effects had become, if anything depoliticizing. Just as purely formal avant garde experiment proved perfectly well suited to grace the homes of conservative bankers, and Surrealist montage to become the language of the advertising industry, so did poststructural theory quickly prove the perfect philosophy for self-satisfied liberal academics with no political engagement at all.

If nothing else this would explain the obsessive-compulsive quality of the constant return to such heroic moments. It is, ultimately, a subtle form of conservatism – or, perhaps one should say conservative radicalism, if such were possible – a nostalgia for the days when it was possible to put on a tin-foil suit, shout nonsense verse, and watch staid bourgeois audiences turn into outraged lynch mobs; to strike a blow against Cartesian Dualism and feel that by doing so, one has thereby struck a blow for oppressed people everywhere.

About the concept of immaterial labor

THE NOTION OF immaterial labor can be disposed of fairly quickly. In many ways it is transparently absurd.

The classic definition, by Maurizio Lazzarato is that immaterial labor is "the labor that produces the informational and cultural content of the commodity." Here, "informational content" refers to the increasing importance in production and marketing of new forms of "cybernetics and computer control," while "cultural content" refers to the labor of "defining and fixing cultural and artistic standards, fashions, tastes, consumer norms, and, more strategically, public opinion," which, increasingly, everyone is doing all the time.[1] Central to the argument is the assertion that this sort of labor has become central to contemporary capitalism, in a way that it never was before. First, because "immaterial workers" who are "those who work in advertising, fashion, marketing, television, cybernetics, and so forth" are increasingly numerous and important; but even more, because we have all become immaterial workers, insofar as we are disseminating information about brand names, creating subcultures, frequenting fan magazines or web pages or developing our own personal sense of style. As a result, production – at least in the sense of the production of the *value* of a commodity, what makes it something anyone would wish to buy – is no longer limited to the factory, but is dispersed across society as a whole, and value itself thus becomes impossible to measure.

To some degree all this is just a much more sophisticated Leftist version of the familiar pop economic rhetoric about the rise of the service economy. But there is also a very particular history, here, which goes back to dilemmas in Italian workerism in the '70s and '80s. On the one hand, there was a stubborn Leninist assumption – promoted, for instance, by Negri – that it must always be the most "advanced" sector of the proletariat that makes up the revolutionary class. Computer and other information workers were the obvious candidates here. But the same period saw the rise of feminism and the Wages for Housework movement, which put the whole problem of unwaged, domestic labor on the political table in a way that could no longer simply be ignored. The solution was to argue that computer work, and housework were really the same thing. Or, more precisely, that they were becoming so: since, it was argued, the increase of labor-saving devices meant that housework was becoming less and less a matter of simple drudgery, and more and more itself a matter of managing fashions, tastes and styles.

The result is a genuinely strange concept, combining a kind of frenzied postmodernism, with the most clunky, old-fashioned Marxist material determinism. I'll take these one at a time.

---

1 "Immaterial Labor" (http://www.generation-online.org/c/fcimmateriallabour3.htm).

Postmodern arguments, as I would define them at least, pretty much always take the same form:

1) begin with an extremely narrow version of what things used to be like, usually derived by taking some classic text and treating it as a precise and comprehensive treatment of how reality actually worked at that time. For instance (this is a particularly common one), assume that all capitalism up until the '60s or '70s really did operate exactly as described in the first two or three chapters of volume I of Marx's *Capital*.

2) compare this to the complexities of how things actually work in the present (or even how just one thing works in the present: like a call center, a web designer, the architecture of a research lab).

3) declare that we can now see that lo!, sometime around 1968 or maybe 1975, the world changed completely. None of the old rules apply. Now everything is different.

The trick only works if you do not, under any circumstances, reinterpret the past in the light of the present. One could after all go back and ask whether it ever really made sense to think of commodities as objects whose value was simply the product of factory labor in the first place. What ever happened to all those dandies, bohemians, and flaneurs in the 19th century, not to mention newsboys, street musicians, and purveyors of patent medicines? Were they just window-dressing? Actually, what about window dressing (an art famously promoted by L. Frank Baum, the creator of the *Wizard of Oz* books)? Wasn't the creation of value always in this sense a collective undertaking?

One could, even, start from the belated recognition of the importance of women's labor to reimagine Marxist categories in general, to recognize that what we call "domestic" or (rather unfortunately) "reproductive" labor, the labor of creating people and social relations, has always been the most important form of human endeavor in *any* society, and that the creation of wheat, socks, and petrochemicals always merely a means to that end, and that – what's more – most human societies have been perfectly well aware of this. One of the more peculiar features of capitalism is that it is not aware of this – that as an ideology, it encourages us to see the production of commodities as the primary business of human existence, and the mutual fashioning of human beings as somehow secondary.

Obviously all this is not to say that nothing has changed in recent years. It's not even to say that many of the connections being drawn in the immaterial labor argument are not real and important. Most of these however have been identified, and debated, in feminist literature for some time, and often to much better effect. Back in the '80s, for instance, Donna Haraway was already discussing the way that new communication technologies were allowing forms of "home work" to disseminate throughout society. To take an obvious example: for most of the twentieth century, capitalist offices have been organized according to a gendered division of labor that mirrors the organization of upper-class households: male executives engage in strategic planning while female secretaries were expected to do much of the day-to-day organizational work, along with almost all of the impression-management, communicative and interpretive labor – mostly over the phone. Gradually, these traditionally female functions have become digitized and replaced by computers. This creates a dilemma, though, because the interpretive elements of female labor (figuring out how to ensure no one's ego is bruised, that sort of thing) are precisely those that computers are *least* capable of performing. Hence the renewed importance of what the post-workerists like to refer to as "affective labor." This, in turn, effects how phone work is being reorganized, now: as globalized, but also as largely complementary to software, with interpretive work aimed more at the egos of customers than (now invisible) male bosses. The connections are all there. But it's only by starting from long-term perspectives that one can get any clear idea what's really new here, and this is precisely what a post-modern approach makes impossible.

This last example brings us to my second point, which is that very notion that there is something that can be referred to as "immaterial labor" relies on a remarkably crude, old-fashioned version of Marxism. Immaterial labor, we are told, is labor that produces information and culture. In other words it is "immaterial" not because the labor itself is immaterial (how could it be?) but because it produces immaterial products. This idea that different sorts of labor can be sorted into more material, and less material categories according to the nature of their product is the basis for the whole conception that societies consist of a "material base" (the production, again, of wheat, socks and petrochemicals) and "ideological superstructure" (the production of music, culture, laws, religion, essays such as this). This is what has allowed generations of Marxists to declare that most of what we call "culture" is really just so much fluff, at best a reflex of the really important stuff going on in fields and foundries.

What all such conceptions ignore what is to my mind probably the single most powerful, and enduring insight of Marxist theory: that the world does not really consist (as capitalists would encourage us to believe) of a collection of discrete objects that can then be bought and sold, but of actions and processes. This is what makes it possible for rich and powerful people insist that what they do is somehow more abstract, more ethereal, higher and more spiritual, than everybody else. They do so by pointing at the products – poems, prayers, statutes, essays, or pure abstractions like style and taste – rather than the process of making such things, which is always much messier and dirtier than the products themselves. So do such people claim to float above the muck and mire of ordinary profane existence. One would think that the first aim of a materialist approach would be to explode such pretensions – to point out, for instance, that just as the *production* of socks, silverware, and hydro-electric dams involves a great deal of thinking and imagining, so is the production of laws, poems and prayers an eminently material process. And indeed most contemporary materialists do, in fact, make this point. By bringing in terms like "immaterial labor," authors like Lazzarato and Negri, bizarrely, seem to want to turn back the theory clock to somewhere around 1935.[2]

---

2   Lazzarato for example argues that "the old dichotomy between 'mental and manual labor,' or between 'material labor and immaterial labor,' risks failing to grasp the new nature of productive activity, which takes the separation on board and transforms it. The split between conception and execution, between labor and creativity, between author and audience, is simultaneously transcended within the 'labor process' and reimposed as political command within the 'process of valorization'" (Maurizio Lazzarato, "General Intellect: Towards an Inquiry into Immaterial Labour," http://www.geocities.

(As a final parenthetical note here, I suspect something very similar is happening with the notion of "the biopolitical," the premise that it is the peculiar quality of modern states that they concern themselves with health, fertility, the regulation of life itself. The premise is extremely dubious: states have been concerned with promulgating health and fertility since the time of Frazerian sacred kings, but one might well argue it's based on the same sort of intellectual move. That is: here, too, the insistence that we are dealing with something entirely, dramatically new becomes a way of preserving extremely old-fashioned habits of thought that might otherwise be thrown into question. After all, one of the typical ways of dismissing the importance of women's work has always been to relegate it to the domain of nature. The process of caring for, educating, nurturing, and generally crafting human beings is reduced to the implicitly biological domain of "reproduction," which is then considered secondary for that very reason. Instead of using new developments to problematize this split, the impulse seems to be to declare that, just as commodity production has exploded the factory walls and come to pervade every aspect of our experience, so has biological reproduction exploded the walls of the home and pervade everything as well – this time, through the state. The result is a kind of sledge hammer approach that once again, makes it almost impossible to reexamine our original theoretical assumptions.)

The art world as a form of politics

THIS RELUCTANCE TO question old-fashioned theoretical assumptions has real consequences on the resulting analysis. Consider

---

com/immateriallabour/lazzarato-immaterial-labor.html. Note here that (a) Lazzarato implies that the old manual/mental distinction *was* appropriate in earlier periods, and (b) what he describes appears to be for all intents and purposes exactly the kind of dialectical motion of encompassment he elsewhere condemns and rejects as way of understanding history (or anything else): an opposition is "transcended," yet maintained. No doubt Lazzarato would come up with reasons about why what he is arguing is in fact profoundly different and un-dialectical, but for me, this is precisely the aspect of dialectics we might do well to question; a more helpful approach would be to ask how the opposition between manual and mental (etc) is *produced.*

Negri's contribution to the conference. He begins by arguing that each change in the development of the productive forces since the 1840s corresponds to a change in the dominant style of high art: the realism of the period 1848-1870 corresponds to one of the concentration of industry and the working class, impressionism, from 1871-1914, marks the period of the "professional worker," that sees the world as something to be dissolved and reconstructed, after 1917, abstract art reflects the new abstraction of labor-power with the introduction of scientific management, and so on. The changes in the material infrastructure – of industry – are thus reflected in the ideological superstructure. The resulting analysis is revealing no doubt, even fun (if one is into that sort of thing), but it sidesteps the obvious fact that the production of art *is* an industry, and one connected to capital, marketing, and design in any number of (historically shifting) ways. One need not ask who is buying these things, who is funding the institutions, where do artists live, how else are their techniques being employed? By defining art as belonging to the immaterial domain, its materialities, or even its entanglement in other abstractions (like money) can simply be sidestepped.

This is not perhaps the place for a prolonged analysis, but a few notes on what's called "the art world" might seem to be in order. It is a common perception, not untrue, that at least since the '20s the art world has been in a kind of permanent institutionalized crisis. One could even say that what we call "the art world" has become the ongoing management of this crisis. The crisis of course is about the nature of art. The entire apparatus of the art world – critics, journals, curators, gallery owners, dealers, flashy magazines and the people who leaf through them and argue about them in factories-turned-chichi-cafes in gentrifying neighborhoods... – could be said to exist to come up with an answer to one single question: what is art? Or, to be more precise, to come up with some answer other than the obvious one, which is "whatever we can convince very rich people to buy."

I am really not trying to be cynical. Actually I think the dilemma to some degree flows from the very nature of politics. One thing the explosion of the avant garde did accomplish was to destroy the boundaries between art and politics, to make clear in fact that art was always, really, a form of politics (or at least that this was always one thing that it was.) As a result the art world has been faced with the same fundamental dilemma as any form of politics: the impossibility of establishing its own legitimacy.

Let me explain what I mean by this.

It is the peculiar feature of political life that within it, behavior that could only otherwise be considered insane is perfectly effective. If you managed to convince everyone on earth that you can breathe under water, it won't make any difference: if you try it, you will still drown. On the other hand, if you could convince everyone in the entire world that you were King of France, then you would actually be the King of France. (In fact, it would probably work just to convince a substantial portion of the French civil service and military.)

This is the essence of politics. Politics is that dimension of social life in which things really do become true if enough people believe them. The problem is that in order to play the game effectively, one can never acknowledge its essence. No king would openly admit he is king just because people think he is. Political power has to be constantly recreated by persuading others to recognize one's power; to do so, one pretty much invariably has to convince them that one's power has some basis other than their recognition. That basis may be almost anything – divine grace, character, genealogy, national destiny. But "make me your leader because if you do, I will be your leader" is not in itself a particularly compelling argument.

In this sense politics is very similar to magic, which in most times and places – as I discovered in Madagascar – is simultaneously recognized as something that works because people believe that it works; but also, that only works because people do not believe it works only because people believe it works. This why magic, from ancient Thessaly to the contemporary Trobriand Islands, always seems to dwell in an uncertain territory somewhere between poetic expression and outright fraud. And of course the same can usually be said of politics.

If so, for the art world to recognize itself as a form of politics is also to recognize itself as something both magical, and a confidence game – a kind of scam.

Such then is the nature of the permanent crisis. In political economy terms, of course, the art world has become largely an appendage to finance capital. This is not to say that it takes on the nature of finance capital (in many ways, in its forms, values, and practices, is almost exactly the opposite) – but it is to say it follows it around, its galleries and studios clustering and proliferating around the fringes of the neighborhoods where financiers live and work in global cities everywhere, from New York and London to Basel and Miami.

Contemporary art holds out a special appeal to financiers, I suspect, because it allows for a kind of short-circuit in the normal process of value-creation. It is a world where the mediations that normally intervene between the proletarian world of material production and the airy heights of fictive capital, are, essentially, yanked away.

Ordinarily, it is the working class world in which people make themselves intimately familiar with the uses of welding gear, glue, dyes and sheets of plastic, power saws, thread, cement, and toxic industrial solvents. It is among the upper class, or at least in upper middle class worlds where even economics turns into politics: where everything is impression management and things really can become true because you say so. Between these two worlds lie endless tiers of mediation. Factories and workshops in China and Southeast Asia produce clothing designed by companies in New York, paid for with capital invested on the basis of calculations of debt, interest, anticipation of future demand and future market fluctuations in Bahrain, Tokyo, and Zurich, repackaged in turn into an endless variety of derivatives – futures, options, various traded and arbitraged and repackaged again onto even greater levels of mathematical abstraction to the point where the very idea of trying to establish a relation with any physical product, goods or services, is simply inconceivable. Yet these same financiers also like to surround themselves with artists, people who are always busy making things – a kind of imaginary proletariat assembled by finance capital, producing unique products out of for the most part very inexpensive materials, objects said financiers can baptize, consecrate, through money and thus turn into art, thus displaying its ability to transform the basest of materials into objects worth far, far more than gold.

It is never clear, in this context, who exactly is scamming whom.[3] Everyone – artists, dealers, critics, collectors alike – continue to

---

3   That is, within the art world. The fact that increasing numbers of the these complex financial instruments are themselves being revealed to be little more than scams adds what can only be described as an additional kink.

pay lip service on the old 19th century Romantic conception that
the value of a work of art emerges directly from the unique genius
of some individual artist. But none of them really believe that's all,
or even most, of what's actually going on here. Many artists are
deeply cynical about what they do. But even those who are the
most idealistic can only feel they are pulling something off when
they are able to create enclaves, however small, where they can
experiment with forms of life, exchange, and production which
are – if not downright communistic (which they often are), then
at any rate, about as far from the forms ordinarily promoted by
capital anyone can get to experience in a large urban center – and
to get capitalists to pay for it, directly or indirectly. Critics and
dealers are aware, if often slightly uneasy with the fact that, the
value of an artwork is to some degree their own creation; collectors, in turn, seem much less uneasy with the knowledge that in
the end, it is their money that makes an object into art. Everyone
is willing to play around with the dilemma, to incorporate it into
the nature of art itself. I have a friend, a sculptor, who once made
a sculpture consisting simply of the words "I NEED MONEY", and
then tried to sell it to collectors to get money to pay the rent. It
was snapped up instantly. Are the collectors who snap up this sort
of thing suckers, or are they reveling in their own ability to play
Marcel Duchamp?[4]

Duchamp, after all, justified his famous "fountain," his attempt
to buy an ordinary urinal and place it in an art show, by saying
that while he might not have made or modified the object, he had
"chosen" it, and thus transformed it as a concept. I suspect the full
implications of this act only dawned on him later. If so, it would at
any rate explain why he eventually abandoned making art entirely
and spent the last forty years of his life playing chess, one of the
few activities that, he occasionally pointed out, could not possibly
be commodified.

Perhaps the problem runs even deeper. Perhaps this is simply
the kind of dilemma that necessarily ensues when one two in-
commensurable systems of value face off against each other. The

4   As a coda to the story, the New Museum in New York, which eventually came into possession of the piece, a few years later put an image
of the sculpture on handbag that it sells in its gift-shop. It has sold
quite well, but the artist has received nothing in the way of reim-
bursement.

original, romantic conception of the artist – and hence, the very idea of art in the modern sense – arose around the time of industrial revolution. Probably this is no coincidence. As Godbout and Caille have pointed out, there is a certain complementarity. Industrialism was all about the mass production of physical objects, but the producers themselves were invisible, anonymous – about them one knew nothing. Art was about the production of unique physical objects, and their value was seen as emerging directly from the equally unique genius of their individual producers – about whom one knew everything. Even more, the production of commodities was seen as a purely economic activity. One produced fishcakes, or aluminum siding, in order to make money. The production of art was not seen as an essentially economic activity. Like the pursuit of scientific knowledge, or spiritual grace, or the love of family for that matter, the love of art has always been seen as expressing a fundamentally different, higher form of value. Genuine artists do not produce art simply in order to make money. But unlike astronomers, priests, or housewives, they do have to sell their products on the market in order to survive. What's more, the market value of their work is dependent on the perception that it was produced in the pursuit of something other than market value. People argue endlessly about what that "something other" is – beauty, inspiration, virtuosity, aesthetic form – I would myself argue that nowadays, at least, it is impossible to say it is just one thing, rather, art has become a field for play and experiment with the very idea of value – but all pretty much agree that, were an artist to be seen as simply in it for the money, his work would be worth less of it.

I suspect this is a dilemma anyone might face, when trying to maintain some kind of space of autonomy in the face of the market. Those pursuing other forms of value can attempt to insulate themselves from the market. They can come to some sort of accommodation or even symbiosis. Or they can end up in a situation where each side sees itself as ripping the other off.

What I really want to emphasize though is that none of this means that any of these spaces are any less real. We have a tendency to assume that, since capital and its attendant forms of value are so clearly dominant, then everything that happens in the world somehow partakes of its essence. We assume capitalism forms a total system, and that the only real significance of any apparent alternative is the role it plays in reproducing that system. Myself, I feel this logic is deeply flawed – and politically disastrous. For two hundred years at least, artists and those drawn to them have created enclaves where it has been possible to experiment with forms of work, exchange, and production radically different from those promoted by capital. While they are not always self-consciously revolutionary, artistic circles have had a persistent tendency to overlap with revolutionary circles; presumably, precisely because these have been spaces where people can experiment with radically different, less alienated forms of life. The fact that all this is made possible by money percolating downwards from finance capital does not make such spaces "ultimately" a product of capitalism any more than the fact a privately owned factory uses state-supplied and regulated utilities and postal services, relies on police to protect its property and courts to enforce its contracts, makes the cars they turn out "ultimately" products of socialism. Total systems don't really exist, they're just stories we tell ourselves, and the fact that capital is dominant now does not mean that it will always be.

On Prophecy and Social Theory

Now, THIS IS hardly a detailed analysis of value formation in the art world. Really it is only the crudest sort of preliminary sketch. But it's already a thousand times more concrete than anything yet produced by theorists of immaterial labor.

Granted, Continental theory has a notorious tendency to float above the surface of things, only rarely touching down in empirical reality – an approach perhaps first perfected by Jean Baudrillard, who could write whole essays where all the agents and objects were abstractions ("Death confronts The Social") and presumably half the fun is supposed to be trying to figure out what – if anything – this might actually mean for anyone's actual life. But Baudrillard, by the end of his life, was essentially an entertainer. This work purports to be more serious. Lazzarato has a particularly annoying habit of insisting his concepts emerge from a large body of recent "empirical research" – research which he never, however, cites or specifically refers to. Negri tends to throw everything, all the specific gestures, exchanges, and transformations into a kind of giant blender called "real subsumption" – whereby since everything is labor, and all forms of labor operate under the logic of capital, there's rarely much need to parse the differences between one form and another (let alone analyze the actual organization of, say, a collection agency, or the fashion industry, or any particular capitalist supply chain.)

But in another sense this criticism is unfair. It assumes that Negri and Lazzarato are to be judged as social theorists, in the sense that their work is meant primarily to develop concepts that can be useful in understanding the current state of capitalism or the forms of resistance ranged against it, or at any rate that it can be judged primarily on the degree to which can do so. Certainly, any number of young scholars, in Europe and America, have been trying to adopt these concepts to such purposes, with decidedly mixed results. But I don't think this was ever their primary aim. They are first and foremost prophets.

Prophecy of course existed long before social theory proper and in many ways anticipated it. In the Abrahamic tradition that runs from Judaism through Christianity to Islam, prophets are not simply people who speak of future events. They are people who provide revelation of hidden truths about the world, which may include knowledge of events yet to come to pass, but need not necessarily. One could argue that both revolutionary thought, and critical social theory, both have their origins in prophecy. At the same time, prophecy is clearly a form of politics. This is not only because prophets were invariably concerned with social justice. It was because they created social movements, even, new societies. As Spinoza emphasized, it was the prophets who effectively produced the Hebrew people, by creating a framework for their history. Negri has always been quite up front about his own desire to play a similar role for what he likes to call "the multitude." He is less interested in describing realities than in bringing them into being. A political discourse, he says, should "aspire to fulfill a Spinozist prophetic function, the function of an immanent desire that organizes the multitude."[5] The same could be said of theories of immaterial labor. They're not really descriptive. For its most ardent proponents, immaterial labor is really important because it's seen to represent a new form of communism: ways of creating value by forms of social cooperation so dispersed that just about everyone could be said to take part, much as they do

5 *Empire*, p. 66.

in the collective creation of language, and in a way that makes it impossible to calculate inputs and outputs, where there is no possibility of accounting. Capitalism, which is reduced increasingly to simply realizing the value created by such communistic practices, is thereby reduced to a purely parasitical force, a kind of feudal overlord extracting rent from forms of creativity intrinsically alien to it. We are already living under Communism, if only we can be made to realize it. This is of course the real role of the prophet: to organize the desires of the multitude, to help these already-existing forms of communism burst out of their increasingly artificial shackles. Besides this epochal task, the concrete analysis of the organization of real-life supermarkets and cell phone dealerships and their various supply chains seems petty and irrelevant.

In contrast the main body of social theory as we know it today does not trace back to such performative revolutionary gestures, but precisely, from their failure. Sociology sprang from the ruins of the French revolution; Marx's Capital was written to try to understand the failure of the revolutions of 1848, just as most contemporary French theory emerged from reflections on what went wrong in May '68. Social theory aims to understand social realities, and social reality is seen first and foremost as that which resists attempts to simply call prophetic visions into existence, or even (perhaps especially) to impose them through the apparatus of the state. Since all good social theory does also contain an element of prophecy, the result is a constant internal tension; in its own way as profound as the tension I earlier suggested lay at the heart of politics. But the work of Negri and his associates clearly leans very heavily on the prophetic side of the equation.

On the fullness of time

AT THIS POINT I think I can return to my initial question: why does one need an Italian revolutionary philosopher to help us think about art? Why does one call in a prophet?

By now, the answer is much less far to seek. One calls in a prophet because prophets above all know how to speak compellingly about their audience's place in history.

Certainly, this is the role in which Negri, Bifo, and the rest have now been cast. They have become impresarios of the historical moment. When their work is invoked by artists or philosophers, this is largely what they seem to be looking for in it. When they are brought on stage at public events, this is mainly what is expected of them. Their job is to explain why the time we live in is unique, why the processes we see crystallizing around us are unprecedented; different in quality, different in kind, from anything that has ever come before.

Certainly this is what each one of the four, in their own way, actually did. They might not have had much to say about specific works of art or specific forms of labor, but each provided a detailed assessment of where we stood in history. For Lazzarato the significant thing was that we had moved from a society of discipline to one of security; for Revel, what was really important was the move from formal to real subsumption of labor under capital. For Bifo, we had moved from an age of conjunction to one of connection; for Negri, the new stage of contemporaneity that had replaced post-modernism. Each dutifully explained how we had entered into a new age, and described some of its qualities and implications, along with an assessment of its potential for some sort of radical political transformation,

It's easy to see why the art world would provide a particularly eager market for this sort of thing. Art has become a world where – as Walter Benjamin once said of fashion – everything is always new, but nothing ever changes. In the world of fashion, of course, it's possible to generate a sense of novelty simply by playing around with formal qualities: color, patterns, styles, and hemlines. The visual arts have no such a luxury. They have always seen themselves as entangled in a larger world of culture and politics. Hence the a permanent need to conjure up a sense that we are in a profoundly new historical moment, even if art theorists attempting such an act of conjuration often seem to find themselves with less and less to work with.

There is another reason, I think, why revolutionary thinkers are particularly well suited to such a task. One can come to understand it, I think, by examining what would otherwise seem to be a profound contradiction in the all of the speakers' approaches to history. In each case, we are presented with a series of historical stages: from societies of discipline *to* societies of security, from conjunction *to* connection, etc. We are not dealing with a series of complete conceptual breaks; at least, no one seems to imagine that is impossible to understand any one stage from the perspective of any of the others. But oddly, all of the speakers in question sub-scribed to the theory that history *should* be conceived as a series of complete conceptual breaks, so total, in fact, that it's hard to see how this would be possible. In part this is the legacy of Marxism, which always tends to insist that since capitalism forms an all-en-compassing totality that shapes our most basic assumptions about the nature of society, morality, politics, value, and almost every-thing else, we simply cannot conceive what a future society would be like. (Though no Marxist, oddly, seems to think we should therefore have similar problems trying to understand the past.) In this case, though, it is just as much the legacy of Michel Foucault,[6] who radicalized this notion of a series of all-encompassing histori-cal stages even further with his notion of epistemes: that the very conception of truth changes completely from one historical peri-od to the next. Here, too, each historical period forms such a total system that it is impossible to imagine one gradually transforming into another; instead, we have a series of conceptual revolutions, of total breaks or ruptures.

All of the speakers at the conference were drawing, in one way another, on both the Marxian and Foucauldian traditions – and some of the terms used for historical stages ("real subsumption," "societies of discipline"...) drew explicitly on one or the other. Thus all of them were faced with the same conceptual problem. How could it be possible to come up with such a typology? How is it possible for someone trapped inside one historical period to be able to grasp the overall structure of history through which one stage replaces the other?

The prophet of course has an answer to this question. Just as we can only grasp an individual's life as a story once he is dead, it is only from the perspective of the end of time that we can grasp the story of history. It doesn't matter that we do not really know what the messianic Future will be like: it can still serve as Archimedean point, the Time Outside Time about which we can know nothing but that nonetheless makes knowledge possible.

Of course, Bifo was explicitly arguing that the Future is dead. The twentieth century, he insisted, had been "century of the future"

6 Really, I would say, it is the legacy of Structuralism. Foucault is re-membered mainly as a post-structuralist, but he began as an arch-structuralist, and this aspect of his philosophy in no sense changed over the course of his career but if anything grew stronger.

(that's why he began his analysis with the Futurists). But we have left that now, and moved on to a century with no future, only precarity. We have come to an point where it is impossible to even imagine projecting ourselves forwards in time in any meaningful way, where the only radical gesture left to us is therefore self-mutilation or suicide. Certainly, this reflected a certain prevailing mood in radical circles. We really do lack a sense of where we stand in history. And it runs well beyond radical circles: the North Atlantic world has fallen into a somewhat apocalyptic mood of late. Everyone is brooding on great catastrophes, peak oil, economic collapse, ecological devastation. But I would argue that even outside revolutionary circles, the Future in its old-fashioned, revolutionary sense, can never really go away. Our world would make no sense without it.

So we are faced with a dilemma. The revolutionary Future appears increasingly implausible to most of us, but it cannot be abolished. As a result, it begins to collapse into the present. Hence, for instance, the insistence that communism has already arrived, if only we knew how to see it. The Future has become a kind of hidden dimension of reality, an immanent present lying behind the mundane surface of the world, with a constant potential to break out but only in tiny, imperfect flashes. In this sense we are forced to live with two very different futures: that which we suspect will actually come to pass – perhaps humdrum, perhaps catastrophic, certainly not in any sense redemptive – and The Future in the old revolutionary, apocalyptic sense of the term: the fulfillment of time, the unraveling of contradictions. Genuine knowledge of this Future is impossible, but it is only from the perspective of this unknowable Outside that any real knowledge of the present is possible. The Future has become our Dreamtime.

One could see it as something like St. Augustine's conception of Eternity, the ground which unifies Past, Present, and Future because it proceeds the creation of Time. But I think the notion of the Dreamtime is if anything even more appropriate. Aboriginal Australian societies could only make sense of themselves in relation to a distant past that worked utterly differently (in which, for instance animals could become humans and back again), a past which was at once unretrievable, but always somehow there, and into which humans could transport ourselves in trace and dream so as to attain true knowledge. In this sense, the speakers at our

conference found themselves cast in the role not even of prophets, perhaps, but of shamans, technicians of the sacred, capable
of moving back and forth between cosmic dimensions – and of
course, like any magician, both a sort of artist in their own right
and at the same time a sort of trickster and a fraud.

Not surprising, then, that as the sincere revolutionaries that
they were, most seemed to find themselves slightly puzzled by
how they had arrived here.

A final note

PERHAPS THIS SEEMS unduly harsh. I have, after all, trashed the
very notion of immaterial labor, accused post-Workerists (or at
least the strain represented at this conference, the Negrian strain
if we may call it that[7]) of using flashy, superficial postmodern arguments to disguise a clunky antiquated version of Marxism, and
suggested they are engaged in an essentially theological exercise
which while it might be helpful for those interested in playing
games of artistic fashion provides almost nothing in the way of
useful tools for social analysis of the art world or anything else. I
think that everything I said was true. But I don't want to leave the
reader with the impression that there is nothing of value here.

First of all, I actually do think that thinkers like these are useful
in helping us conceptualize the historical moment. And not only
in the prophetic-political-magical sense of offering descriptions
that aim to bring new realities into being. I find the idea of a revolutionary future that is already with us, the notion that in a sense
we already live in communism, in its own way quite compelling.
The problem is, being prophets, they always have to frame their
arguments in apocalyptic terms. Would it not be better to, as I
suggested earlier, reexamine the past in the light of the present?
Perhaps communism has always been with us. We are just trained
not to see it. Perhaps everyday forms of communism are really
– as Kropotkin in his own way suggested in *Mutual Aid*, even
though even he was never willing to realize the full implications
of what he was saying – the basis for most significant forms of human achievement, even those ordinarily attributed to capitalism.

---

7   Just to bring my own biases out: I feel much closer, myself, to the
    Midnight Notes strain represented by figures such as Silvia Federici,
    George Caffentzis, or Massimo de Angelis.

If we can extricate ourselves from the shackles of fashion, the need to constantly say that whatever is happening now is necessarily unique and unprecedented (and thus, in a sense, unchanging, since everything apparently must always be new in this way) we might be able to grasp history as a field of permanent possibility, in which there is no particular reason we can't at least try to begin building a redemptive future at any time. There have been artists trying to do so, in small ways, since time immemorial – some of them, as part of genuine social movements. It's not clear that what we are doing when we write theory is all that very different.

Against Kamikaze Capitalism

ON SATURDAY, OCTOBER 16TH, 2010, SOME 500 ACTIVISTS
gathered at convergence points across London, knowing they
were about to embark on a direct action called Crude Awakening,
aimed against the ecological devastation of the global oil industry,
but beyond that, with no clear idea of what they were about to
do. The organizer's plan was quite a clever one. Organizers had
dropped hints they were intending to hit targets in London itself,
but instead, participants – who had been told only to bring full-
charged metro cards, lunch, and outdoor clothing – were led in
brigades to a commuter train for Essex, well outside of the city
limits. At one stop, shopping bags full of white chemical jumpsuits
marked with skeletons and dollars, gear, and lock-boxes mysteri-
ously appeared; shortly thereafter, hastily appointed spokespeople
in each carriage – themselves kept in the dark until the very last
minute – received word of the day's real plan: to blockade the access road to the giant Coryton refinery near Stanford-le-Hope
– the road over which 80% of all oil consumed in London flows.
An affinity group of about a dozen women, they announced, were

already locked down to vans near the refinery's gate and had turned back several tankers; we coming to make it impossible for the police to overwhelm and arrest them.

It was an ingenious feint, and brilliantly effective. Before long we were streaming across fields and hopping streams carrying thirteen giant bamboo tripods, a handful of confused metropolitan police in tow. Hastily assembled squads local cops eventually appeared, and first seemed intent on violence – seizing one of our tripods, attempting to break our lines when we began to set them up on the highway – but the moment it became clear that we were not going to yield, and batons would have to be employed, someone must have given an order to pull back. We can only speculate about what mysterious algorithm the higher-ups apply in such situations – our numbers, their numbers, the danger of embarrassing publicity, the larger political climate – but the result was to hand us the field. Before long our tripods stood across the highway, each topped by an activist in white jumpsuit solemnly silhouetted against the sky. A relief party proceeded down the road to back up the original lockdown. No further tankers moved over that access road – a road that on an average day carries some seven hundred, hauling 375,000 gallons of oil – for the next five hours. Instead, the access road became a party: with music, clowns, footballs, local kids on bicycles, a chorus line of Victorian zombie stilt-dancers, yarn webs, chalk poems, periodic little spokescouncils – mainly, to decide at exactly what point we should declare victory and go home.

It was nice to win one for a change. Faced with a world of dominated by security forces that seem veritably obsessed – from Minneapolis to Strasbourg – with ensuring that no activist should ever leave the field of a major confrontation with a sense of elation or accomplishment, a clear tactical victory is certainly nothing to sneeze at. But at the same time, there was a certain ominous feel to the whole affair – one which made the overall aesthetic, with its mad scientist frocks and animated corpses, oddly appropriate.

Le Havre

THE CORYTON BLOCKADE was inspired by a call from Climate Justice Action network, a new global network created in the lead-up to the actions in Copenhagen in December 2009 – meant to be a kind of anti-Columbus day, called by indigenous people in defense of the earth.[1] Yet it was carried out in the shadow of a much-anticipated announcement, on the 20th, four days later, of savage Tory cuts to the tattered remains of the British welfare state, from pensioner's support, youth centers to education – the largest such since before the Great Depression. The great question on everyone's mind was, would there be a cataclysmic reaction? Even worse, was there any possibility there might not be? Across the channel, the reaction to a similar right-wing onslaught had already begun. French Climate Camp had long been planning a blockade similar to ours at the Total refinery in Le Havre, France's largest, but by the eve of their scheduled action on the 16th, they discovered the refinery had already occupied by its workers as part of a nationwide pension dispute that shut down 11 of Frances 12 oil refineries. Ecoactivists quickly decided to proceed with the action anyway, erected a symbolic blockade, but ended up spending most of the rest of the day in a battle of cat and mouse, their protracted efforts to break through the police cordon to join forces with the workers matched only by the authorities steely determination that the conversation should not take place. (Eventually, some thirteen bicycles did get through.)

"Environmental justice won't happen without social justice," remarked one of the French Climate Campers afterwards. "Those who exploit workers, threaten their rights, and those who are destroying the planet, are the same people." True enough. "The workers that are currently blockading their plants have a crucial power into their hands; every liter of oil that is left in the ground thanks to them helps saving human lives by preventing climate catastrophes."

But were French oil workers really striking for the right to stop being oil workers? At first sight statements like this might seem shocking naïve. But in fact, this is precisely what they were striking for. They were mobilizing around reforms that will move up their retirement age from 60 to 62; and they were manning the barricades, along with large segments of the French population, to insist on their right not to be oil workers one minute longer than they had to.

---

1 Originally set for Tuesday the 12th, the traditional "Columbus day," it was actually a call for a week of actions, and activists in both the UK and France actually carried them out on Saturday the 16th.

We might do well to reflect on the police determination that environmental activists and petroleum workers not sit down together. Surely there is a conversation that needs to take place here; a conversation about the very nature of money, value, work, production, of the mechanics of the global work machine that threatens to destroy the very possibility of sustainable life on this planet. The powers that be are desperate to ensure it never happens. But the fact that workers were striking, not for more money, but, however modestly, however defensively, *against work*, is enormously important.

The productivist bargain and the paradox of the twentieth century

ONE OF THE great ironies of the twentieth century that everywhere, a politically mobilized working class – whenever they did win a modicum of political power – did so under the leadership of cadres of bureaucrats dedicated to a productivist ethos that most of the working class did not share. In the early decades of the century, the chief distinction between anarchist and socialist unions is that the former always tended to demand higher wages, the latter, less hours. The socialist leadership embraced the consumer paradise offered by their bourgeois enemies; yet they wished to manage the productive system themselves; anarchists, in contrast, wanted time in which to live, to pursue (to cast it in perhaps inappropriately Marxian terms) forms of value of which the capitalists could not even dream. Yet where did the revolutions happen? As we all know from the great Marx-Bakunin controversy, it was the anarchist constituencies – precisely, those who rejected consumer values – that actually rose up: the whether in Spain, Russia, China, Nicaragua, or for that matter, Algeria or Mozambique. Yet in every case they ended up under the administration of socialist bureaucrats who embraced that ethos of productivism, that dream of consumer utopia, even though this was the last thing they were ever going to be able to provide. The irony became that the principle social benefit the Soviet Union and similar regimes actually was able to provide – more time, since work discipline becomes a completely different thing when one effectively cannot be fired from one's job – was precisely the one they couldn't acknowledge; it had to be referred to as "the problem of absenteeism" standing in the way of an impossible future full of shoes and consumer electronics. But if you think about it, even here, it's not entirely different. Trade unionists, too, feel obliged to adopt bourgeois terms – in which productivity and labor discipline are absolute values – and act as if the freedom to lounge about on a construction sites is not a hard-won right but actually a problem. Granted, it would be much better to simply work four hours a day than do four hours worth of work in eight, but surely this is better than nothing. The world needs less work.

All this is not to say that there are not plenty of working class people who are justly proud of what they make and do, just that it is the perversity of capitalism (state capitalism included) that this very desire is used against us, and we know it. As a result, it has long been the fatal paradox of working class life that despite working class people and sensibilities being the source of almost everything of redeeming value in modern life – from shish kebab to rock'n'roll to public libraries (and honestly, what has the middle class ever come up anyway?) – they do so precisely when they're *not* working, in that domain that capitalist apologists obnoxiously write off as "consumption." Which allows the remarkably uncreative administrative classes (and I count capitalists among these) to dismiss all this creativity, then, to take possession of it and market it as if it were their own invention.

How to break the cycle? In a way this is the ultimate political question. One of the few things everyone seems to agree with in public discourse on the budget, right now, or really on any kind of class politics, is that, at least for those capable of work, only those willing to submit to will-nigh insane levels of labor discipline could possibly have any right to anything – that work, and not just work, work of the sort considered valuable by financiers – is the only legitimate moral justification for rewards of any sort. This is not an economic argument. It's a moral one. It's pretty obvious that there are many circumstances where, even from an economists' perspective, too much work is precisely the problem. Yet every time there is a crisis, the answer on all sides is always the same: people need to work more! There's someone out there working less than you, a handicapped woman who isn't really as handicapped she's letting on to be, French workers who get to retire before their souls and bodies have been entirely destroyed, lazy porters, art students, benefit cheats, and this must, somehow, be what's really ruining things for everyone.

So, what was neoliberalism?

IN THIS, THE obsession with work is perfectly in keeping with
the spirit of neoliberalism itself, which, in its latter days is becoming increasingly revealed for really always was: that form of
capitalist governance that always places political considerations
ahead of economic ones. As a result it was an ideological triumph
and an economic catastrophe. Neoliberalism was the movement
that managed to convince everyone in the world that economic
growth was the only thing that mattered, even as, under its ae-
gis real global growth rates collapsed, sinking to perhaps a third
of what they had been under earlier, state-driven, social welfare-
oriented forms of capitalism. Neoliberalism was the system that
managed to convince everyone in the world that financial elites
were the only people capable of managing or measuring the value
of anything, even as in order to do so, it ended up promulgating
an economic culture so irresponsible that it allowed those elites
to bring the entire financial architecture of the global economy
tumbling on top of them because of their utter inability to assess
the value even of their own financial instruments. Again, this was
no accident. The pattern is consistent. Whenever there is a choice
between the political goal of demobilizing social movements, or
convincing the public there is no viable alternative to the capitalist
order, and actually running a viable capitalist order, neoliberalism
means always choosing the former.

Almost all its claims are lies. Yet they are startling effective
ones. Precarity is not really an especially effective way of organizing labor. It's remarkably effective way of demobilizing labor.
The same is of course true of constantly increasingly labor-time.
Economically, it's if anything counter-productive (especially if we
imagine capitalists do want to be able to pass on their ill-gotten
gains to their grandchildren); politically, there is no better way
to ensure people are not politically active or aware than to have
them working, commuting to work, or preparing for work every
moment of the day. Sacrificing so many of one's waking hours to
the gods of productivity ensures no one has access to outside perspectives that would enable them to notice – for instance – that
organizing life this way ultimately decreases productivity. As a
result of this neoliberal obsession with stamping out alternative
perspectives, since the financial collapse of 2008, we have been left
in the bizarre situation where its plain to everyone that capitalism

doesn't work, but it's almost impossible for anyone to imagine anything else. The war against the imagination is the only one the capitalists have actually managed to win.

Kamikaze capitalism

IT ONLY MAKES sense, then, that the first reaction to the crash was not – as most activists, including myself, predicted – a rush towards Green Capitalism, that is, an economic response, but rather, a political one. This is the real meaning of the budget cuts. Any competent economist knows where radically slashing spending during a recession is likely to lead. They might pretend otherwise, summoning up obscure formulae to back up their political patrons of the moment, but that's just their job – they know it's a recipe for disaster. The response only makes sense from a political perspective. Financial elites, having shown the world they were utterly incompetent at the one activity they had claimed they were best able to do – the measurement of value – have responded by joining with their political cronies in a violent attack on anything that even looks like it might possibly provide an alternative way to think about value, from public welfare to the contemplation of art or philosophy (or at least, the contemplation of art or philosophy for any other reason than the purpose of making money). For the moment, at least, capitalism is no longer even thinking about its long-term viability.

It is disturbing to know that one is facing a suicidal enemy, but at least it helps us understand what we are fighting for. At the moment: everything. And yes, it is likely that in time, the capitalists will pick themselves up, gather their wits, stop bickering and begin to do what they always do: begin pilfering the most useful ideas from the social movements ranged against them (mutual aid, decentralization, sustainability) so as to turn them into something exploitative and horrible. In the long run, if there is to be a long run, it's pretty much inevitable. In the meantime, though, we really are facing kamikaze capitalism – an order that will not hesitate to destroy itself if that's what it takes to destroy its enemies. It is no exaggeration to speak of a battle between the forces of life and the forces of death here.

How, then, to break the back of the productivist bargain? This is hardly the place to offer definitive answers, but at least we can think about the conversation that needs to be taking place. And it might suggest some directions. It might help to start by acknowledging that we are all workers insofar as we are creative, and resist work, and also refuse to play the role of the administrators – that is, those who try to reduce every aspect of life to calculable value. That means trying to understand the true nature of the global work machine, the real relation of those domains of life artificially separated into "economics," "politics," and "ecology." The relation between oil and money actually provides a striking illustration. How is it that we have come to treat money, which after all is nothing but a social relation, and therefore infinitely expandable, as if it were a limited resource like petroleum ("we must cut social services because we simply don't have the money"), and oil, which actually *is* a limited resource, as if it were money – as something to be freely spent to generate ever-increasing economic activity, as if there would never be an end to it? The two forms of insanity are, clearly, linked.

Really a coin is just a promise, and the only real limit to the amount of money we produce is how many promises we wish to make to one another, and what sort. Under existing arrangements, of course, there are all sorts of other, artificial limits: over who is legally allowed to issue such promises (banks), or determine what kinds of promises have what sort of comparative weight (in theory, "the market," in reality, increasingly bureaucratized systems of financial assessment.) It is such arrangements that allow us to pretend that money is some kind of physical substance, that debts are not simply promises – which would mean that a government's promise to pay investors at a certain rate of interest has no greater moral standard than, say, their promise to allow workers to retire at a certain age, or not to destroy the planet), but as some kind of inexorable moral absolute. Yet it's this very tyranny of debt – on every level – that becomes the moral imperative that forces oil from the earth and convinces us that the only solution to any moral crisis is to convert yet another portion of free human life into labor.

Minor Compositions

Other titles in the series:
Precarious Rhapsody – Franco "Bifo" Berardi
Imaginal Machines – Stevphen Shukaitis
New Lines of Alliance, New Spaces of Liberty – Felix Guattari
and Antonio Negri
The Occupation Cookbook
User's Guide to Demanding the Impossible – Laboratory of
Insurrectionary Imagination
Spectacular Capitalism – Richard Gilman-Opalsky
Markets Not Capitalism – Ed. Gary Chartier & Charles W.
Johnson

Forthcoming:

Communization & its Discontents – Ed. Benjamin Noys
19 & 20 – Colectivo Situaciones
A Very Careful Strike – Precarias a la Deriva
Punkademics – Ed. Zack Furness
Art, Production and Social Movement – Ed. Gavin Grindon
        As well as a multitude to come…

CPSIA information can be obtained at www.ICGtesting.com
Printed in the USA
BVOW071721011111

275013BV00002B/2/P